Personal Note

Reminiscenses & Reflections
on
The Antiquarian Book Trade 1985 – 2015

Julian Nangle

Words Press

Limited Edition of 250 numbered copies,
numbers 1–40 with an extra illustration and signed by the author.

This is no. 142

Edited by Julie Musk
Designed, printed and bound by Joshua Horgan, Oxford

Published by Words Press
25 High East Street
Dorchester DT1 1EZ
www.wordspress.co.uk

ISBN: 978-0-9550931-2-8

INTRODUCTION

I have been publishing catalogues of rare and collectable books since May 1974 when I struck out on my own, having worked for other book dealers and emporiums, including Christie's of St James, Shakespeare & Co in Paris, and the Modern First dealers Bertram Rota, over a period of 7 years. Circumstances fell that come May 1974 I was ready to proceed with the next phase of my bookselling life. My then wife Edith was pregnant with our first child and we had a flat, near Godalming in Surrey, large enough for me to store a thousand or so books. I borrowed £2000 from my parents for my first major purchase, and I was away.

Within 18 months we had moved from the country up to London and had bought an abandoned shop with accommodation above in Theberton Street, which runs between Upper Street and Liverpool Road, in Islington.The shop had been left vacant since 1943 and I had great fun restoring it and converting it into a second-hand bookshop. It was in the basement of this shop in 1976/77 that we held 36 weekly poetry readings, on the trot, without a week missed. Many famous poets came. It was one of the highlights of my life; it was the realisation of a dream, a fantasy even. Ever since I had entered the bookselling world, in 1967, I had wanted to have my own bookshop, to live above it, and to hold poetry readings in it. That I achieved this, at a relatively young age, still astounds me.

In February 1978 Edith left me and I was devastated. The thought of getting up and opening the shop everyday seemed impossible to me. Somehow I got onto a network where I found Lizzie Graves, the niece of the poet Robert Graves, and she came to work for me at the shop and, basically, kept Words Etcetera going during the whole of 1978. For a time, later, when she went to India for a spell, her friend Emma Stone, who, it turned out, was the daughter of another veritable star in the world of books, Reynolds Stone, replaced her and kept the shop's fire burning. I, meanwhile, had retreated upstairs to my accommodation above the shop, where I spent my time reading up on Buddhism and writing endless amounts of poetry. I barely sold a book, personally, during 1978.

And so, fast forwarding to my 50th catalogue in 1985, I found myself wanting to acknowledge Lizzie's help. Without it I don't know what I would have done. It is down to her that I wrote that first Personal Note and, consequently, it is down to her that I have written one in each catalogue issued ever since. The Notes themselves tell most of the story thereafter. I can only hope they prove enjoyable, even interesting, and that they give some background to the ebb and flow within the mind and life of an antiquarian bookseller of the '70s, '80s,'90s and '0ies, and his constant need and desire to maintain a connection with his loyal customers, to whom he extends his sincere and grateful thanks for their patronage over the years.

I have been very strict with myself and tried to leave the Personal Notes much as they were written, with their naivety screaming off the page occasionally, or perhaps commonly – you to judge. The illustrations are, I hope, self-explanatory. The typewriter logo that features on the covers of many of my catalogues in the 1990s was drawn for me by the noted painter Michael Taylor, whose portraits of John Taverner, P.D. James, Julian Bream and others can be viewed at the National Portrait Gallery and other notable institutions or, indeed, online. I feel very lucky to have known Michael at a stage in his career when he would even consider doing such a menial task as a logo for his friend down the road (on two different occasions; he also designed the covers for the series of poetry pamphlets called Mir Poets that my wife Anna and I produced in the late 1980s).

I also wish to take the space here to thank each and every 'subscriber' to this little book. Your names are listed at the back, as promised. Thank you for giving me the confidence to see this venture through to a conclusion that you can actually hold in your hands.

It is well known within the book trade that I have moved dozens of times in the 40 years since I set up on my own. It is perhaps less well known that in that time I opened and closed at least eleven different bookshops, during one period having five shops open at the same time – a mini chain.The reasons for my moves are many and varied, although a common denominator to them has been 'family'. The different needs of the children over the years have instigated many of the moves; simply housing five children under eleven together on a bookseller's budget demanded some imaginative 'out of the box' thinking on more than one occasion. I make no apology for ruining many address books; I have found the nomadic life, which took me to France for a spell, and also to Spain, thoroughly exciting and rewarding.

At times over the years I found myself a little bored with bookselling and ventured into publishing. The first illustration in this book displays the leaflet I produced to announce 'Slightly Soiled' which was an irreverent dig at how 'establishment' I was finding the world of bookselling, especially its ruling body, the ABA. The first issue of SS had a cover illustration by Patrick Hughes depicting a coffin with the letters A B A down the front of it, standing upright at a microphone addressing God knows who. It was meant, and was felt, to be an angry suggestion that those in power in the ABA at that time – the mid 1980's – were not addressing the needs of its rank and file members. In truth I think I was just rebelling against the very being of an institution; something I seem to have done all my life. I blame it on having been a prisoner at boarding school for 11 impressionable years.

I shall stop now, before I turn this Introduction into an autobiography. The autobiography I want you to read awaits, in the shape of these diary entries that I have called Personal Notes. You will notice there are some gaps, that there are some catalogues not listed. This is mainly because I have mislaid copies of these catalogues in my archive. Within those Personal Notes I have elected to keep in there has been some editing, as, inevitably, there is considerable repetition. I have left some of the repetition in as it gives a flavour to the unerring whir of a life committed to reproducing catalogues, one after the other, over 40 years. I am trusting, however, that it does not dominate or overshadow the flow from one Personal Note to the next. *Julian Nangle*

PS. One last thing: anything written in italics represents current 2014/2015 thoughts and comments. I have tried to resist adding too many, but one or two have escaped the blue pencil.

In conclusion I would like to thank my editor, Julie Musk, for her invaluable help in making my utterances intelligible and reasonably consistent. Any errors are mine alone.

'Papa was a rolling stone' designed and hand printed by Poppy Nangle

Words Etcetera

CAT 50
(*The first Personal Note*)
1985

On the occasion of our 50th catalogue I feel it is fitting to acknowledge it with a few words of boasting, reminiscence and thanks.

Eleven years ago, in May 1974, I issued my first catalogue pseudonymously after working for other booksellers for 7 years as a kind of apprenticeship. That first catalogue was of Literary Periodicals priced between 50p and £5.00. Since then, as long-term customers will know, and for whose forbearance I am most grateful, the business has moved no less than five times. That we have moved floors at 327 Fulham Road (and are considering doing so again!) does not shadow my pride for having stayed at the same address for over 2 years and look set to remain for another two.

Just before moving to Fulham Road I employed an assistant, Lucy Cawthron, who has proved more helpful and supportive than any employer ever could have expected. Much of Words Etcetera's apparent stability must be lain at her door.

Between 1975 and 1980 my ex-wife and I ran a bookshop in Theberton Street, Islington. Its opening made some impact, being written up in the *Evening Standard*, *Time Out* and even the *Highbury & Islington Gazette*. It was a shop of great character, we were assured by many who visited it, and if I have one regret it is that I do not still have the premises. Over a period of as many weeks we had 36 nationally known poets come and read in the basement, including the current (and I trust long-standing) Poet Laureate. I would like to take this extremely belated opportunity to thank the London Poetry Secretariat for their financial support and in particular Olwen Ellis for her help. The readings would never have happened without both.

Lucy Cawthron is not the first assistant to Words Etcetera. That dubious honour went to Lizzie Graves who worked in the shop during 1978 and helped me through a very difficult patch.

No 'review' of Modern First Editions selling over the past decade can ignore the leap in values and change in importance of condition. This phenomenon has come directly from the United States. I remember vividly, on my first trip to the States in 1978, the staggering array of rare and beautifully preserved books to be seen on the shelves of the West Coast booksellers. The situation has not changed there, but their insistence on fine condition has infected us all, collector and seller, to varying degrees. Words Etcetera, to try to place us on the grid, would always consider buying and selling a copy of *Miguel Street* by V.S. Naipaul without its jacket, whereas C.P. Snow's *Homecomings* would only be of interest fine in jacket. However, there are some booksellers who would not want *Miguel Street* unless it was in dust-wrapper, which Words Etcetera feels is a little extreme. There are many people wanting the book, and not all of them wishing to pay £250 for it, however fine.

Enough politesse though: prices have rocketed and with them the game has become a very serious one, with people cashing in wherever and in whatever guise they can. I think this is a pity, but then who gives a damn? I suppose the day has gone when a collector relies on one bookseller for all his acquisitions, and while this is sensible from the collector's point of view, it makes life cut-throat for the booksellers. Please do not think I am complaining though – if the kitchen gets too hot I *will* get out, but it's not too hot yet and I trust I'll be able to write another piece of self-indulgence as introduction to our catalogue 100.

Meanwhile I should like to come to my most important point: thank you, customers, for buying the books you have over these past 11 years – may this catalogue tempt you sufficiently to permit us to issue many, many more.

CAT 52
Late Summer 1985

Imagine you have spent every conceivable spare moment in your working life on your pet project. It is not in the mainstream of your work since it does not render sufficient financial rewards, but it matters to you.

Next imagine that the fruit of your labours has finally ripened to maturity and is presentable to the grapefruit market out there. You wait for the reviews and reactions.

Imagine now that you receive a telephone call or letter asking for the most insignificant particle from the fruit, for a pip or a sliver of its peel. This is flattering, in the sense that any reaction to one's labours is flattering (remember Wilde's delight at people talking negatively behind his back?) But it is equally if not more frustrating when one reflects that the juice and core of the fruit have been ignored.

This is the feeling I shall have should somebody ring up and order an item, shall we say value £1 or £2, on its own. Flattered but frustrated. My apologies in advance if there is such an item herein for you, but I must warn you that I might be tempted to overlook such an order. Time spent thus would be hard to justify.

CAT 57
Winter 1986

With this catalogue I have reduced the mailing list significantly. Everyone who receives this has either ordered from me at one time or another or requested a catalogue be sent to them relatively recently (within the last 6 months). If you are among the latter and do not order from this or the following two catalogues you will automatically be removed from the mailing list – sorry !

For those who might be remotely interested, I am living an ecstatic life down in the country, nipping as many dead rose heads as I am cataloguing books. The quality of life, it seems to me, is down to the emphasis we choose to put on its different compartments. If we concentrate ourselves in the city which the majority of the western world seems economically and socially obliged to do we inevitably become distanced from the nature of life. With the advent of computer-communication leaving the necessity to 'go to work' standing in the hall with its hat half on, I foresee, thankfully, a large-scale return to the countryside. Commuters will become a thing of the past, British Rail will have to look around for another Beeching, communities and community living will reappear with a gusto not seen since flower power, the world will be back on course. For this reason alone I am thrilled beyond measure that the technological age has brought us the computer, although I, personally, would not be seen dead owning one!

Oh yeah?

CAT 58
Spring 1987

The ecstatic life continues, albeit under a few feet of snow! Four months in brings no regrets, only impatience for the Spring. I have found the furore over the abominable weather this country has suffered recently very telling. To continue where I left off in my last catalogue, I find it reassuring to note that Nature still has the power, in this instance through wind and snow, to return us humans, where ever we may live, to our true nature; viz people offering the old and the poor shelter in their own centrally heated homes while others are snatching the last loaf of bread on the shelf. No one can claim Mankind is anything but enigmatic.

CAT 60 Vol. 1
Summer 1987

This is a large catalogue but it should bear fruit for those who read it. I have reduced prices to the point where I hope a battering ram runs through the ridiculous pricing of Modern Firsts of recent years. It is my firm belief that the trade is far advanced in slitting its own throat unless the razors are blunted. When I began selling Modern Firsts, collecting was not a rich person's hobby exclusively but for all reasonably interested in literature. Over the past few years I feel more and more 'ordinary' collectors have been dropping their interest in collecting as the prices have risen. This is a great shame and this catalogue is my humble attempt to tempt back the regular if modest collector of first editions.

Disenchanted as I have become with my chosen field of Modern Firsts, I am trying to buy earlier books, going back to the 18th century even, on a small scale. If customers have any particular interests (not necessarily literary) in earlier books I hope they will feel inclined to tell me them, for this would help guide me as to what I should catalogue in the future. I shall continue to issue Modern First catalogues, of course, so WANTS in this field are welcome as ever, as in the field of modern engraved books and original wood engravings.

Anyone travelling out of London will be more than welcome in Child Okeford, where, in the garden, hundreds of wild flowers compete with rambling roses, and other flowers whose names I do not know, for the eye of the panicking gardener as onlookers and passers-by tap him on the hoe saying, "There, there, Winter'll come soon an' do the jarb for ye". Just get a train to Gillingham and see it for yourself. And you can look at the books here, too.

CAT 61
Early Autumn 1987

This is becoming something of a tradition which I hesitate to continue since you are not on my mailing list to receive the thoughts of Bookseller Nangle but to see if you can't find an elusive rarity or, at least, a book you have long wished to own and/or read. However, the response to my little outbursts has been so extraordinarily warm and positive that I shall dare to delay your entry into the catalogue proper for as long as the postman refrains from delivering unwanted raspberries. At this time, when the leaves are busy preparing their farewells from their parent trees, it seems appropriate to mutter a few words about a new business I have started. It is called the Tree Sanctuary. The idea, in brief, is to offer anyone wanting one a tree sanctuary of their own. I am hoping to have a leaflet printed in time to send out with this catalogue, but if I fail to do this anyone wishing to receive it need only phone up and ask for it or write in for it. Basically, the Tree Sanctuary is offering the chance to purchase a quiet spot and plant a tree of your own choice on it. You will then have a rural retreat all your own.

CAT 64
Summer 1988

This catalogue boasts a rather smarter cover than usual in celebration of the mid-summer mad-week of June where book people traditionally become possessed to become dispossessed of their money. If you are picking this catalogue up at the ABA Book Fair please do feel free to write or ring if there is anything within it that interests you. I send out regular catalogues, although not always chock-a-block with inscribed or signed books as this one is.

I am constantly looking for individual books and libraries of fine-condition rare modern first editions. This description may sound a little obvious, but my observations suggest that fewer and fewer good rare modern first editions are about. I have done several sweeps through country bookshops and have been sadly amazed at how little good quality modern firsts there are, even to look at, let alone ponder on buying.

Am I alone in this observation? America! Have you got the lot?

Looking through the contents of this catalogue has frightened me. There are so many books that (a) I do not remember owning and (b) according to my marked copy of the catalogue did not sell! I will give two examples, mouth-watering as they are.

Item 9 offered: Francis Bacon. Bacon. Text by Sir John Rothenstein. Masters Series 71. 1967. SIGNED PRESENTATION COPY FROM THE ARTIST. £150.00

Item 193 offered: Philip Larkin. Jill. INSCRIBED BY THE AUTHOR 'To Bruce, in memory of Shropshire and Oxford, and with love and sincere thanks for encouraging this book. Philip. Leicester, 1946'. 1946. [Bruce Montgomery, better known as Edmund Crispin, was Larkin's closest friend in the early days of his literary career.] £1100.00

I suspect today both books would have an extra 0 added to their price, but where are they?

CAT 66
Winter 1988

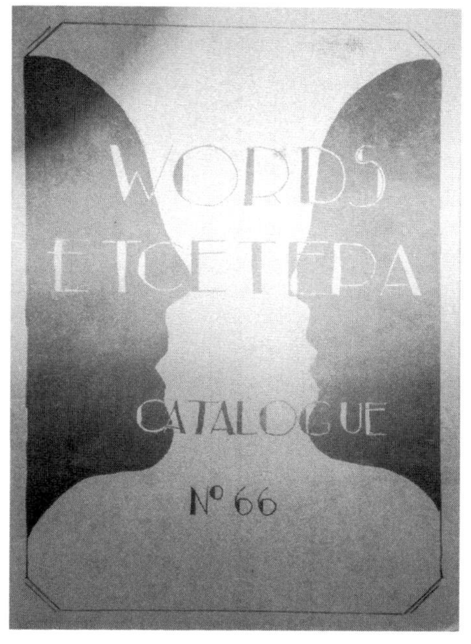

Some kind, sensitive customers made me feel positively wanted by their mourning the absence of a Personal Note in Catalogue 65. And it wasn't that I'd not written one – I had, but my printers (though they claim it were I) LOST it! Well, if I want this catalogue printed the less said about that the better (but they won't lose this one will they?)

This catalogue has the rare distinction of having a cover designed by my 13-year-old daughter. She is studying Craft and Design at school so thought a little practical experience wouldn't be a bad thing. I had to agree with her. At the back of the catalogue you'll notice I have listed Words Press publications. If you ever wanted a bargain look no further. The R.S. Thomas, Andrew Motion, James Merrill collectors have been plundering the Words Press reserves with a ferocity and enthusiasm unmatched in the Press' short history. So don't get left out; as the advertisers would say "Hurry, hurry, hurry!"

I don't feel particularly angry about anything as I sit at the typewriter attempting to sound interesting. For the last couple of years I've managed to identify, trap and expel certain bees from my bonnet, but November 1988 finds me surprisingly tranquil, suspiciously becalmed of the winds of opinion. Unless somebody whispers the word 'Media' in my ear and then, of course, my sails will ruffle until full blown and I will tell you how appalling I find the whole concept of mass communication (as I have done on several earlier occasions). Anyway, I'd need another ocean of white paper, not just another paragraph or page, to distill the reasons that our egocentric beings are so in need of being told of the troubles of others less fortunate than ourselves. Perhaps the human species needs to feel guilty, oppressed and utterly useless. But no, no, I scream, for I don't.

CAT 67
Early Spring 1989

The countryside this winter has seemed like a poor version of the Cote d'Azur. We've had one frost all winter. Well, one of any note. Christmas passed off smoothly which was a relief, although there was one incident in the village which became the talking point whenever two villagers bumped into each other round one or other of the two corners on the main street here. The sheep! Whose dog is killing the sheep? Our Hambledon Hill is an ancient fortified hill of great anthropological importance (Cromwell himself is said to have conquered it – as he did Corfe Castle not so far away), so to have a dog ravaging four sheep on the trot as we have is nothing less than a village scandal. And yet it's all gone suspiciously quiet on that front – perhaps it was the farmer's own dog? I did hear one utterance of such unmentionable rumour.

CAT 69
Summer 1989

The flowers are out and so is the sun. The radio blathers on about why we should and why we shouldn't be closer to Europe. China is manifesting enormous change. Meanwhile I ponder on my membership of another club, bigger than any nation (even China) or any union of nations (even Europe), and consider what is being done to safeguard it. I speak, of course, of the Planet.

The Greenhouse Effect, the Ozone Layer, but two new terms firmly established in the language now, but how many of us know exactly what they mean? I have made an effort to get to know but still balk at the idea of passing on such information I've gleaned in case I've got it wrong!

Seriously, however, such vanities must be put aside. We live in an age where the Planet is threatened and threatened truly. The apathy and complacency exhibited by the litter lout or the property developer is hard to take. Out here in the country the developer, particularly, sticks in my gullet. Some land in the village, recently sold for development, lay secret behind a wonderful ancient hedge which, on the first morning the bulldozers arrived, was ripped out of the ground – a hedge that has probably been there about 100 years summarily obliterated in 1 hour. It takes some swallowing that, and some understanding. Perhaps we should desist from referring to the Planet as Mother Earth and call her, instead, Mummy Earth. Everywhere I look all I see are screaming children demanding THEIR sweetie from the fast withering hand of the once held sacred Planet Earth, the place we call 'home'. I wonder for how long ....

Recently I came across Thomas Hardy's poem 'Throwing a Tree' (published in Winter Words) in which the last line reads: "And two hundred years' steady growth has been ended in less than two hours".

CAT 70
Autumn 1989

I hope you have had a pleasant summer. My summer was mixed. I bought some nice books in London and then went on holiday with my children (two of my own and three 'step'). We went to Antibes and stayed there, without moving, since to move meant treading on someone, for 6 days. We then went inland to a camp site near to Avignon where we experienced desert survival. I have never been so hot for so long in my life. There was not a tree over 20 days old and the swimming pool was the size of my daughter's bandana. Thankfully we headed for Avignon town to catch the night train home but had to wait over 9 hours pottering around the Palais de Papes, with the two youngest children, boys aged six and eight, choosing to turn the vast banqueting hall into a boxing arena. We quickly threw in the towel and escaped through Pope Benedict's ante chamber to the real world of rip-off lunches and serenading 'I want you to think I'm an orphan' urchins. The prize for my greatest waste of money goes to Arles not Avignon, however; 7 croissants plus a drink each: £14.50.

CAT 71
Winter 1989

Half term is coming to an end, so there is room in the house once again. The box of Lego has been returned to beneath the youngest's bed, the Brio stored away in the cupboard under the stairs – an innocent enough act you might think, but what chaos it brought. The cupboard under the stairs (I wonder why someone has not compiled an anthology of stories featuring this most exciting and mysterious of places) is also host to the Christmas decorations. Ben, our 6-year-old resident mouse/little boy, discovered them when returning his toys at the end of his playathon lasting the entire half term. Naturally he was drawn to the chocolate decorations which Woolworths and the like produce every Christmas to stimulate even greater sales of tooth-decaying yummies. Unfortunately, for little boys of six, the mere fact that these chocolates had sat there in the dark unmolested for a year was of no consequence, so he quaffed the lot, leaving a trail of silver paper up the stairs all the way to the bathroom, where, I presumed, he was going to regurgitate the stale bonbons down the lavatory. Not a bit of it – he'd merely moved on to the final chore of the day – washing his teeth.

Six hours later, at approximately 2.00 am, we were awoken by a piercing scream. Ben was having a nightmare. His mother settled him, only to be awoken at 4.00 am by a low groaning howl. Ben was having another nightmare. The moral for us adults became clear over breakfast: try not to let your children eat chocolate last thing at night, and heaven help you if it is last year's chocolate. Still, they're (almost) all back at school now and safely under other people's control, which is just the way I like them when they are at that 'exploratory' phase. The garden has been blown away, hence absence of comment thereon.

CAT 72
Early Spring 1990

The number of this catalogue is highly significant. From earliest times, the number 72 has been known to have magical qualities. The original draughtsmen of the New Jerusalem Diagram, which is the symbol of divine order on earth (and by God don't we need it!), showed us that all the significant measurements, or virtually all, were multiples of number 72. A few examples: the Earth's diameter (7920 miles) is 72 × 110; the Moon's diameter (2160 miles) is 72 × 30; the Sun's diameter (864,000 miles) is 72 × 12,000; Earth–Moon distance (237,600 miles) is 72 × 3300; Earth–Sun distance (93,312,000 miles) is 72 × 1,296,000. This is just the start of a fascinating labyrinth which begins to be unravelled by John Michell in his book *The Dimensions of Paradise*. When you think about it, number 72 has to be kind of special when the number 12 (a significant number in itself – apostles, months, hours, the New Jerusalem's 12 gates, pearls, foundations, names, jewels and angels as outlined in St John's revelation) is multiplied by its own half, 6, and produces 72, which, amazingly again, is the number that the word Truth in Greek adds up to, so long as you are using any normal lexicon. The word Jesus, by the same methods, for example, adds up to 888. And we all know about 666, the Beast.

Anyway, enough of this; anyone interested in the subject should get John Michell's book (Thames & Hudson, 1988). Meanwhile, I trust you may find plenty to interest you within the catalogue; the books are as cheap as I can reasonably make them, I hope you will agree.

CAT 74
Summer 1990

This page is looking like a printer's manual. I hope the change in typefaces has not lost you before you've entered the catalogue itself! The reason for it is to draw attention to our NEW TELEPHONE NUMBER. This number will be answered between normal business hours but NOT otherwise. Outside normal hours it will turn into a monstrous ansa-phone. For the purpose of clarity, I shall spell out my 'normal business hours' as being 10.00 am – 6.00 pm Monday–Friday. If customers wish to reach me personally I might still be found on the old phone number, but would prefer not to be unless truly URGENT! To save you reading between these lines I can explain this change by advising that I have moved my office out of my home but will continue to receive all mail at home and all phone calls at the office. I will not confuse the situation any further by furnishing customers with my office address – it is not of consequence to anyone but myself! Suffice to say I shall only be personally available on the phone between 10.00

and 6.00 Monday–Friday, and not always then. I have to go out and LOOK for books occasionally! Hope you like these ....

CAT 75
Autumn 1990

I am fighting against the temptation to get political in this space. Listening to Dean Martin crooning 'Everybody loves somebody sometime' is straining my throat muscles to their limit, they want to throw up all over him, and to get the vocal chords working to the same tune but with the words 'No one really gives a damn for no one!' Still, that's where my politics must stop, now, instantaneously. There is NOTHING more boring than reading about a bookseller's political views, EVEN when the world is poised to throttle itself. No, no, it's useless; I will continue on my rural Dorset way and tell you about Bonnie, our brand new Border Collie pup of 4 months 2 weeks and 3 days who is great! I didn't know what living in the country was until I got a dog – now I don't know what being at home is since I'm never there, I'm always dodging the cow pats and medicated water troughs (NO politics remember) and keeping VERY firmly to the rights of way across every farmer in the neighbourhood's land! It's great fun seeing how slowly I can walk while keeping this bundle of unrestrained energy in view, for it is SHE who wishes to remain in view, nervous of what the wonderful world of rabbit droppings and, God willing, an actual rabbit, could inflict on an intuitive (for she is nothing less). I watch that TV programme *One Man and his Dog* with a new verve, on the edge of my seat with the absolute knowledge that one day that will be ME up there in the Welsh hills whistling backwards to get my Bonnie to go forwards. ... Hope you like the books within ....

CAT 76
Winter 1990

For the first time ever I am writing this Personal Note on my computer, which seems a contradiction in terms but there we are. This catalogue is larger than most recent ones I've issued and full of what I hope will be considered modestly priced books.

After having gone over the top about my dog in the last catalogue I am feeling very nervous of saying anything at all. I go for long walks accompanied by you know who and compose great odes, which one day will be collected and offered in some bookseller's catalogue for a princely sum. Actually I do believe creativity is a threatened species, not just because some governments don't support the arts as they might but because the way of life today encourages us to ignore our own, our very own, creativity, which is always with us and only needs our attention for us to experience it. So often I find the pressures of everyday life, stupidly paid attention to by my mind, supersede the gentler demands of my creativity. Well, no longer! If the next thing you receive from me is not a catalogue but a mythological tale you will know why. Happy Christmas.

CAT 76 has to be a contender for my most embarrassing PN!

CAT 77
Spring 1991

This has been a curious catalogue to compile insofar as it has found me introducing a new aspect to my catalogue description – that of the attributable blurb. Some of these blurbs have been especially solicited by the publishers, some are from reviews of the edition from the other side of the Atlantic; whatever the source, I felt they were present in such numbers that they commanded mention. One or two came as surprises, such as Salman Rushdie 'blurbing' Geoff Dyer's 1989 novel *The Colour of Memory.* There is a John Fowles jacket blurb I cannot at present locate in the catalogue – hunt the thimble, Fowles collectors! – which again struck me as a little incongruous.

The outlook in the book trade, like in the world, has its clouds in the sky, but I'm off to the San Francisco book fair as soon as I've put this catalogue to bed and intend to enjoy myself there. I hope you might be able to summon up some enthusiasm for what is to be found within these pages despite the continuing depressing world news.

The weather forecast for the next 3 days is 'copious snow fall', which is very exciting if a little poorly timed for my journey to Gatwick. However, feast your imaginative eye on the fields of Dorset turned white for a moment and see a black Border Collie with a white throat hurtling round her beleaguered owner (who is stuffed into a duffle coat) in ever-increasing circles. Here you have the picture of your bookseller studiously at work. Nice work ... when you can get it.

CAT 78
Early Summer 1991

Struggle as I do I cannot help but feel depressed. The world seems to be full of displaced persons: Kurds, Tibetans, Middle East hostages. Hostages all, but to what? Not to fortune, that's for sure. My feeling is that if we could all contract ourselves a bit, and begin to see that the world, the real world, the world of that genius Carl Gustav Jung, begins and ends with ourselves, the world 'out there' would be a better place by half. All tumult seems to flow from self-aggrandisement (look at Saddam, look at Hitler, look at every tin-pot dictator in history) and I have a sneaking feeling that this was what the late, great Graham Greene was on about.

In fact, his death, only 3 days ago as I write, is the REAL reason for my low feelings. With his leaving I feel there's not much point staying on at the party. Oh dear, oh dear, how I must be conveying this all to you, patient customer, I do apologise. Perhaps this summer I shall live in honour of all those who have served humanity faithfully while resisting the temptation to get all 'puffed up'. GG takes the salute as I march past, every time.

CAT 79
Summer 1991

I've just heard from somebody doing the Park Lane Hotel ABA Book Fair that it is not going as well as he might have hoped – that it is quiet. Well, I feel terrible about this. I was meant to share his stand with him but pulled out 4 months before the event, to be told by the ABA that I had left it 'very late'. I had a lot on this summer – still do. Anna and I are getting married on August 10th! And one way or another, the ABA Fair didn't stay at the top of my priorities. There's another one planned for November at the Chelsea Town Hall and I have found myself responding very warmly to that, though the ABA may not respond to my application so warmly of course – we shall see! There is something I have grown to dislike about the

June Fairs – they feel like a subterranean current that you defy at your peril, and that leaves me feeling like the bull that's been thrust into the ring to find El Cordobes shoving a red towel in my face. Consequently, I have all but denied the fairs, visiting the second PBFA one at the Russell on the last day for about 3 hours.

To be honest, I find it increasingly hard to leave the lush green swathes of Dorset for the filthy over-peopled streets of the city, but then I've never been a particular fan of Johnson. Living down here gives me the opportunity to stare at this computer screen for as long as I can take it and then, within ten minutes, be at the foot of an Iron Age fortified hill, rumoured to have been conquered by Cromwell, all set to conquer it myself!

This catalogue is going out to many, many more people than usual. I hope it may prove of interest to a good number of you, and that, whatever the hills you choose to conquer in life, you will have a good summer in the sun with a tree proffering shade to lean against, to read your bounty culled from this catalogue.

CAT 80
Winter 1991

This catalogue has been a long time coming, but here it is, not quite all I'd intended it to be, since I have a large store of periodicals I'd hoped to include which for various reasons I could not. If you are particularly interested in contributions to periodicals do let me know and I could quote you some.

That said I want only to wish every one of you a Happy Christmas, assuming I can afford the staggering airmail costs of sending the overseas catalogues by air. Still, life's been very good for me this year and I hope it hasn't been too bad for you – I got married, as announced in my last catalogue (thank you for your good wishes), I had a lovely family holiday in Cornwall albeit of only a week, and I'm all set to spend 3 days in a relaxing health farm prior to Christmas, since all five of the dear offspring will have gone off to their respective 'other parent'!

I have spent the day, unusually for me, speaking to no one. I have seen no-one and spoken to no-one but the dog, and to her only gruffly. I feel like a character out of Roald Dahl's book *The BFG*, one of those slobbering unfriendly giants who you approach with great wariness and then only in a helicopter.

Anna and I recently went to the Boston Book Fair, which was fine, but the hotel we stayed in, which will remain nameless, had a strange side order available: touch electricity. We couldn't switch a light or open a door without adding to our voltage holdings. This was so much the case by the third day that when we gave each other a brief kiss in the lobby we both jumped a foot backwards, electrified by the experience!

CAT 81
Early Spring 1992

I'm having far fewer copies of this catalogue printed than normal, not because it's full of periodicals but because 1500 people I sent the last two catalogues to didn't reply. So all of you who are receiving this have been in touch with me in the past year, I think. And thank you!

This has been a labour of love, not of business. Indeed, as the recession's teeth finally reach the quick of Dorsetshire it has felt close to suicidal of me to persist, but love is stronger than fear. I don't know if it has been a common phenomenon but I found the month of January to be a singularly bad one, with everything that could go wrong going wrong. I even had a car crash – something that's not happened to me for 21 years. The bio-rhythms were decidedly 'anti' in January, but a friendly astrologer I know told me that "The aspects changed on Feb 3rd", so we're out of it, thank God. So relax, peruse, and purchase and dig the spring.

Talking of spring, the first snowdrops are out in our garden and the daffodil bulbs are bursting their bounty. Any day now we'll be enfolded by yellow, which will certainly be a change from the turgid grey and mud-spattered dark green which the lanes around here have boasted all winter. Fare well.

CAT 82
Spring 1992

Everything, it is said, goes in cycles. This is a most reassuring assertion, which is underlined at this time of year when the daffodils scream their yellow at me and I grudgingly suppose the sun will shine sometime in the following few months.

The problem, as I see it, isn't the cycles of Nature but the cycles of one particular component of Nature; a component that has, until recently, assumed itself above or outside Nature: Man. Both in America and Britain we are involved in just such a cynical event right now – the election of our 'leaders'. I wonder if ants have such a custom ... I don't believe they do.

One species of animal that certainly does NOT elect its leader is the dog. I can say this with warm and delicious certainty since I elected myself leader over my dog some 18–20 months ago now. She has remained entirely faithful to my whims and fancies too, despite my recently letting her off the lead in a leafy, quiet lane of Child Okeford. This is a most dangerous thing to do I have realised. Thirty yards round the corner the Water-Board had mounted their annual excavation. The inevitable result was that I came by some minute and a half later to find Bonnie (who supposedly should have raced past it at 60 mph and by now be at the second gate waiting for me) struggling herself free of the last inches of water-clogged mud which emanated from what can only be described as an open well. You can imagine how she looked and I felt! 'A rat' probably covers both of us. But we survived, as we shall survive the next few weeks/months of political engineering. May you, treasured customer, survive intact also, to enjoy further stretches of uninterrupted, imaginative reading. I vote for: THE BOOK.

CAT 83
Summer 1992

As I sit down to write this I have the summer sound of Radio Three cricket commentary humming in the background. For us in England the last days have been like the South of France, with waves of warm days bathing us in lethargic illusions that we need not work, really. I went off to a camp with my family recently where the 'Travellers' and their wonderful 'vehicles' were much in evidence. These are people I have some respect for since they are not driven by what most of us in the West are driven by, namely security and comfort. 'Travellers' live for the day, which is certainly a goal I share but fail to achieve with any regularity. Nonetheless, their lifestyle leaves them as vulnerable to abuse as does the more conservative chase for money, as you will appreciate when I tell you that three of my children were offered 'mushrooms' as they wandered around the tie-dye market stalls which looked like a rainbow bazaar. The youngest child innocently looked up into the eyes of this drug pusher and said "No thank you, I don't like mushrooms", by which I trust the salesman was suitably dumb-struck.

For Water Board watchers I can report that the hole into which my dog Bonnie temporarily disappeared on a walk back in February/March is still there! Don't fret, you too can get to Child Okeford in time to fall in it should you so wish. I haven't seen a work-person (I'm an Equal Opportunities Employer) anywhere near this hole, deep, wet and murky as it is, ever since it was dug. A mushroom to the person who can give the answer to the question: What are they … doing?

The books in this catalogue are a slightly different mix to my usual. You will see a good number of illustrated items. I must say I do find them more substantial than the ultra-modern first edition, but that's my personal taste. I suppose I'm hoping that it might be yours. Whether it is or not I wish you a good summer, but I wonder, Gooch has just run himself out. Bad omen, bad omen.

CAT 84
Early Autumn 1992

Since I set up in business on my own I have not known the mood of the business of bookselling so dark. I suppose it has to be expected after the broad smiles of the 1980s that there be such dour doldrums in the '90s, but I can't, for the life of me, see the reason for it. I'm sure in England the whole business is linked to house prices. Certainly since the value of my house has fallen regularly over the past 3 years I have begun to wonder how to stop the rot and began by editing my own personal expenditure. This is what the recession is, isn't it? If the value of my house was to start rising again I have no doubts that the level of my expenditure would follow suit and people like me, in business on their own, could start to breathe normally again.

I have been waiting for one or two giants in the trade to fall over. It hasn't happened yet, unless you count George's Rare Book Dept selling up. It is all a bit depressing, but I am very conscious of contributing to its continuance by moaning on about it so I shall stop and start moaning about my holiday, which, until the very last day (down near Carcassonne in the Languedoc region of France), was bliss personified. My wife and I plus six children (our five plus eldest's boyfriend) were happy languishing by the pool in a campsite near Trebes and returning in the evening to this glorious house loaned to us by some dear friends originally met through BOOKS. But then we had to leave. This was enough to ruin our holiday in itself, but added to this we lost three suitcases off our roof rack south of Nantes (safely recovered), only to lose another one (without noticing because we'd stuffed the previously perilously perched ones INSIDE the back of the car) and spent 2 hours running around Rennes in 35°C looking for a police station to report the loss (for insurance purposes). Well, we finally managed all that and went on to Cherbourg in the now pouring rain, to find we couldn't, as we'd hoped, get on an earlier boat and would have to camp overnight in Cherbourg, in the aforementioned rain. We did, we got wet, we left. And here we are, trying to earn our living again so we can repeat the whole exercise next year!

CAT 85
Winter 1992

You will find enclosed in the catalogue an envelope addressed to myself. The purpose of this enclosure is for you to jot down your TOP TEN WANTS and mail them to me. This done I will make a concerted effort to trace some of them. I don't really want 'anything by', but specific books; I have found it singularly unsuccessful trying to meet 'anything by' requests. If you don't have anything specific just now I can wait, but if you do and would be pleased to receive quotes on them use the envelope please.

You will also notice that my address has changed. In fact I've returned to an office I had a couple of years ago, since, pending a couple of crucial negotiations, we have sold our house and will be moving into rented accommodation for a while.

I have recently learnt that not everyone understands the purpose of a code-word so I will merely emphasise that I have one for use in telegrams or Tele-messages or whatever they have now. To send a message saying Spring 242 would mean "Please send from catalogue 85 item 242". It's cheaper, that's all. In case I don't manage to get another catalogue out until Christmas, let me be the first, etc. ….

CAT 86
Early Spring 1993

Am I pleased it's 1993! Over the Christmas fortnight I and my family were involved in One Christmas, One House Move, Two Car Crashes and Three Birthdays. Each of the crashes involved one of my daughters – the first one had me driving (too fast for the conditions, I readily admit) and could so easily have killed us both. Terrifying. The second was less terrifying for those concerned but more devastating in as much as the car concerned was written off. This concerned my eldest daughter and her boyfriend in his car at the grand old speed of 25 mph. The eighteenth birthdays of these two love birds happen to be a day apart – December 29th and December 30th – and the shocking introduction to the hardnosed world of insurance occurred on the first of these birthdays. Meanwhile the rest of the family was doing its best to settle into a brand new home which is just a mile away from the office!

So, every day, when the weather is kind enough, I WALK to the office with dear Bonnie, who could lead me from door to door with my eyes closed should she need to. The walk is wonderful because half of it is down a private tree-lined drive which happens to be a public footpath, so I am able to FEEL if not BE a most widely landed gent for quarter of an hour every morning. Once the dark evenings finish I'll walk home too, but for the moment the treat is just watching the new appearance of snowdrops and crocuses each morning beneath the trees. Happy Spring.

CAT 87
Spring 1993

I know I have a reputation for being a peripatetic bookseller and possibly one who can't spell long words, but I'm on the move AGAIN, if things go according to plan. I anticipate this will be as permanent a move as the move from London to Hod House was, i.e., for a good 6 years! Famous last words I know. This new move will be operative from May or June, depending on the efficiency of lawyers, so I won't trouble you with the new address just yet. The main reason for this move is quite straight-forward, however. My wife Anna qualified as a McTimoney Chiropractor in November last year and, since we like to work within the same galaxy, we decided that it would be best to move house to accommodate her practice rather than for her to go off and find some distant and costly 'rooms'. The only problem with this plan was the housing market and its 'slowness', to say the least. Consequently we both moved our businesses out of the home, sold the home very quickly, to our astonishment, have been living in temporary accommodation since Christmas and are now poised, having found the right property, to move into a house which will also serve as a business base. Hence the imminent change of business address yet again, for which apologies. I trust, however, that I explained the situation in a manner you can understand.

Incidentally, for anyone out there who has not encountered McTimoney Chiropractic I can thoroughly recommend it. I was a guinea-pig for 3 years while Anna trained and I can guarantee its effectiveness in the business of relieving muscular and nerve pain, not to mention the poor old back! In response to this catalogue, please carry on as before. I shall be alerting all the various agencies to forward mail, transfer phone calls, etc. automatically, should I move before I manage to get out another catalogue, which I think is rather likely. Meanwhile may I wish you all a good, warm, sunny summer.

CAT 88
Summer 1993

It's Royal Ascot. It's the first day of the Second Test in the Ashes series. It's the day before the first day of the June Book Fairs jamboree in London and it is not raining. Tomorrow, we are promised, it will be raining, in time for Wimbledon which starts in 3 days. No one could say the summer in England is uneventful.

To throw my hat, in the form of this catalogue, into this melee might be considered presumptuous. I humbly concede the potential for this view but would urge any who take it to peruse the listing of books I offer. They will see that no summer can be spent sensibly without acquiring at least one of these fascinating volumes.

Please note my new phone number, fax and address where I and my family are very happily ensconced. This is an idyllic house surrounded by a garden which comprises an apple and pear orchard and sundry beautiful rose bushes. As anyone who knows about gardening will tell you from this description, it is an easy garden to maintain.

CAT 89
Early Spring 1994

It has been a while since I sent out a catalogue. It may have been as long ago as last July. The reasons for this are manifold, but the chief among them is that I am bookselling less and less and developing a practice in psychotherapy more and more. I apologise to those who may have missed the regularity of my catalogues and I must warn them that this state of affairs is likely to become more the norm not less.

Even so, I submit what I hope may be a tempting offering of little jewels particularly rich, in this particular catalogue, in literary periodicals. I also enclose a card for those of you who feel moved to let me have your Top 10 Wants. I am still out and about a good amount and may well be able to find what it is you are seeking, so do let me know what it is you are looking for just now. I regret that it has been my experience that tracing particular issues of journals is hard slog for little reward; however, contributors to journals is another matter. If you are collecting an author to the depths of contributions to periodicals I would be extremely keen to help you. Indeed it is what I most enjoy about bookselling. I love the transience of the poem or article that first appears in some forgotten journal – I'm thinking of the example offered in this catalogue under Louis MacNeice*– so easily overshadowed by the 'First Book' of an author. Some of these pieces, offered here, are uncollected. Surely this makes their serendipity value priceless and

their allure irresistible? I hope to get another catalogue out later this year, maybe in the summer, but until I do I wish you a very happy, peaceful and prosperous New Year.
** the poem 'Salute!' which appears in Socialist Review Vol 1 No 1 (c. 1939) and was offered at £45.*

CAT 90
Spring 1994

This catalogue is a particularly personal one. It was put together largely by my daughter, Olivia, eager for work in her year out after leaving school last summer before going to Cambridge this autumn. She raided my loft space and came up with this lot, or a lot of it!

Ever since I sent out my first catalogue, almost 20 years ago to the day, I have been a bit of a hoarder of correspondence. My father taught me never to throw away a piece of string if it could be used a second time; indeed he must have been one of the pioneers of recycling, now I come to think of it. And so it was that I rarely threw away a letter from somebody if I had heard of them in some context beyond their writing to me.

Putting values on such things is difficult, of course, even for the seasoned trader in such things, for the very reason that they are personal. I have tended to evaluate the letters in the spirit of it being nice to have something original from the hand of the writer one is interested in. I have evaluated the archives from the more objective perspective of seeing them in the light of everything else that's been going on in the Small Press world over the same period. Words Press has not been a major player, and I have not put major prices on the archives. But it did have its niche, especially during the 1970s.*

To have my daughter catalogue my recent history has been a strangely gratifying experience. I hope the fruits of her labour might prove an interesting read if not a temptation to pick. In fact what I REALLY hope is that they might prove both.

I AM working on the many Wants sent in from the last catalogue, for which many thanks. I hope to become more and more active in my 'searching' capacity. If you don't hear from me within a month or so it'll mean the books are horrendously hard to find, something you probably know already! Meanwhile I wish everyone in the northern hemisphere a great Spring and those in the south a great Autumn.

* *Looking through the catalogue I see there were 160 lots devoted to the Words Press archive. Such treasures as Wilfrid Blunt's original typescript for an article of his I published in the second issue of a literary magazine entitled Words Etcetera, in 1971, with autograph corrections in his hand, offered, and snapped up, for the princely sum of £20.00. There were also author-corrected typescripts by George Mackay Brown and Andrew Motion, and letters, some autograph and some typed, from Ted Hughes, Tom Stoppard, R.S. Thomas, Alan Sillitoe, James Merrill, Kathleen Raine, David Gascoyne, Ruth Fainlight, Brian Patten, Thom Gunn, Allen Ginsberg, and so it goes on. What was I thinking? I was thinking: I need money!*

CAT 92
Autumn 1994

I've opened a shop. After 14 years, for some extraordinary reason, I decided to return to the equivalent, in bookselling terms, of Zorba's 'catastrophe': shop, lease, staff, everything, the full catastrophe! But strangely it isn't a catastrophe, at least not yet and I have been open only 3 weeks. Anyone within spitting distance should come down and take a look. I'm open Monday–Saturday 9.30–5.30, and until the end of October and from Easter next year through to October I'll be open Sundays from 10–4.

If you have a shop I believe you should try to keep it open, unlike one I visited only last week where the opening hours stated on the door that they would open at 11 o'clock. By 11.20 I was on to my third coffee (having arrived at 10.00 imagining maybe that they would keep sensible hours). By 11.30 I realised I would have to leave as I was due in Exeter at 12.30, so I went, resolved to resist any urge to return.

If, when ordering, you get a voice you are unfamiliar with, please be patient for it will be my staff learning their ropes. The address of the shop is 6 WEST STREET, BLANDFORD FORUM, DORSET. But please continue using the same old address above for all postal matters.

CAT 94
February 1995

Preparing this catalogue late on Sunday evening, as I am, you may imagine my demeanour after encountering two of the teenagers in my house swapping horror stories about the various colours of gunge that emanates from their noses once they remove the studs pierced through this perfectly innocent part of their anatomy in a mad, at least in my mind, frenzy last summer, or was it longer ago than that? "Why remove the studs?" you might quite reasonably enquire; indeed why put them in in the first place would be an even more reasonable enquiry. Back to the original problem though; why remove the studs, especially since the process of putting them in was so excruciatingly painful (oh yes, we heard about that in graphic detail too!)

Here the younger generation has us over a barrel, it appears, as the teachers will not permit them to wear their nose studs in school – at least certain teachers will not permit it – hence the necessity to learn the art of speedy and discreet removal – hence the various colours of gunge. If you haven't – don't – that is – don't ask any question whatsoever as to why your teenage son or daughter does ANYTHING that they do, the explanation is invariably three times as ghastly as the act itself.

After this short and involuntary burst of autobiography I can only apologise for it and make small recompense by offering you a huge catalogue* of diverse and generally interesting books. The most interesting, to my mind, is the sumptuous edition of *Aesop's Fables* illustrated and signed by Bewick (Item 185**). This book is not typical of my stock, at least it hasn't been in the past, but I very much hope to stock more of this kind of thing in the future. Too long have I remained in the narrow gully of the 20th century.

If you are in the neighbourhood I hope you might feel tempted to make the extra detour and come by Blandford Forum – it is described by Pevsner as being the finest existing example of a Georgian town in England – how can you even THINK of just going to the giant Tesco Cathedral being built on the bypass, and miss experiencing the finest existing example of Georgian England now proudly represented (in part) by Words Etcetera bookshop at 6 West Street?

* *1342 items*

** *Bewick was priced £650*

CAT 95
April 1995

No! We haven't moved again so don't reach for that filing card – we have, instead, expanded! There are now two shops in Dorset, at the addresses above*. There is also a very small shop in Brighton. The address of that one is UPSTAIRS AT PRINNY'S, 3 MEETING HOUSE LANE, THE LANES, BRIGHTON, and it is open Monday–Saturday 9.30–5.00. The shop in Dorchester is considerably larger than Blandford, having 12 other booksellers renting shelf space from us on the first floor– well worth a visit if you're down our way. Blandford also has some dealers renting shelf space, three in all, so it won't just be Words Etcetera you visit when you come to the shops.

Dorchester opened to great attention and with great success on Saturday April 1st. Since then it has been consistently busy. In the week that followed the opening, I believe the first time there was absolutely nobody browsing in the shop was 7 days later, half an hour before the Grand National was off!

All the books in this catalogue are on the shelves at Dorchester, so if you wish to inspect any of them 'come on down'. Hope I might see you there or in Blandford or, very occasionally, in Brighton.

* *Blandford and 2 Cornhill, Dorchester*

CAT 96
June 1995

This catalogue is jam-packed with good old traditional first editions – there will be no headings such as 'Architecture' or 'Mexican interest' which you may have noticed have been creeping into the last few catalogues reflecting the kinds of books I've been offered across the counter in the shops by Joe Public. This collection is just the first of several I hope to put out over the next few months, from an out and out collector of modern first editions. All the books, save those sold from the shelves of the shops between today and getting the catalogue printed and out to you, are on view at the Blandford shop.

Cataloguer of these books: Pete Scott.

Happy Summer.

CAT 98
September 1995

The heat we have been labouring under these past 2 months is beginning to get to me. I am off on holiday in 3 days' time and tempting fate just a bit by secretly, entirely to myself, willing it to rain for a couple of days at the start so that I may recover from this incessant struggle which we go in for in Britain, namely battling the elements with tweezers and tooth-picks when pitch-forks are called for. Air conditioning as a concept has not yet reached Dorset and of course we never expect this kind of heat to go on, and on, and on, so when it does we just fry. It is the same in winter when it snows; gravel the roads? – no, it'll be melted by morning ....

This morning I took my Border Collie Bonnie for a walk down by the river. Inspired by a programme on TV last night about inhabitants of the northernmost village of the world who stand over an ice-hole waiting for up to 3 hours, motionless, for a seal to appear, at which point they shoot it, I stood and stared into the river, aware of the wild life living, loving and feeding from this gentle and undemanding environment. I was excited to see minnows in the surprisingly clear water, defined even more clearly because of the sun, dappled by low-lying boughs. I became ecstatic, later, when I saw the tell-tale long shadows of really, and I mean, really weighty looking fish cruising the still, brown, clear water under the lee of the further bank. I cursed my pitiful ignorance of the countryside that I couldn't tell whether these were trout, carp, bream or maybe even pike, but to see them, to watch them for minutes at a stretch, alone with my dog, was an experience I will not forget.

I hope this catalogue finds you in a spirit of rest and relaxation – it should do, it's the summer holidays! How exciting!

CAT 99
Autumn 1995

Another catalogue, fast on the heels of the last, brings with it my good wishes and news that in the Blandford shop we are currently having a SALE of modern first editions. There are a good 1001 first editions which are for sale at 50% off the marked price. So hurry on down and I'll see you there!

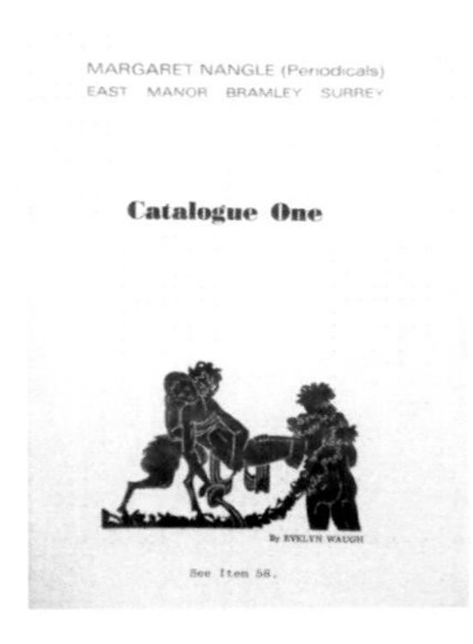

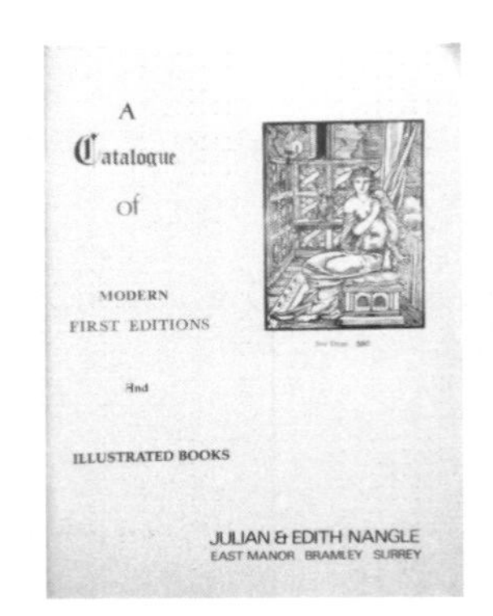

CAT 100
Winter 1995

Catalogue 100. Who'd have thought it way back in May 1974 when I sent out Catalogue 1 (as if from my mother Margaret Nangle, due to a logistics problem resolved by the time Catalogue 2 was issued), my first child, Olivia, who is about to be 21 this Christmas, not yet born. I vividly remember taking an order from an American university for some issues of *Horizon* magazine for the mighty sum of £2.25. Things certainly have changed. I won't labour any nostalgic points, but I do think it might be the moment to thank all of YOU who have stayed my customers throughout these past 21 years. Now it is time to raise our glasses.

CAT 101
Feb/March 1996

Since issuing the last catalogue much has happened. Sadly, on January 23rd, my mother died. She traded in books herself, as Margaret Nangle Children's Books. I feel very pleased she saw me reach my century of catalogues. As I write this the snow is falling, but I feel pretty good about that since I have been confined to bed for a couple of days trying to overcome the second if not third onslaught of flu. It has been a particularly tenacious strain of flu this year which releases you, only to come back within a week or two. Ah well, enough about health, or the lack of it. I am

off for a short break in the sun before sending this catalogue out and so trust you will find me refreshed and raring to go to meet any forthcoming orders. May Spring and/or some kind of 'feel-good' factor come early for you this year.

CAT 1
New Series
Summer 1996

With this catalogue I am shedding my trading name for the purposes of catalogues. Words Etcetera continues to exist, as a thriving bookshop* housing 18–20 booksellers' stock displayed on two floors at the above address. If you haven't visited this emporium yet you are missing out on a delightful experience (or so many of our visitors lead us to believe). However, I wish to differentiate between my business as a bookshop and my business as a mail order bookseller. I'd be grateful therefore if all catalogue orders are to me, Julian Nangle, at the above address.

Meanwhile I would love to tell you about a trip I made to Ireland recently to visit my youngest daughter Poppy who has taken to living in Cork. I say I'd love to tell you because it is not possible in the few lines I have here to describe the extraordinary experiences I encountered in search of the rare book in Ireland, not an easy quest to satisfy. I recommend any serious book scout in Ireland to head for the one shop not listed in the *Guide to Antiquarian and Second-Hand Booksellers in Ireland*, to be found in Bantry trading under the title Nora's Books. Not only did this shop have some interesting books, but also it was open on the Sunday my daughter and I visited Bantry. I was struck in Ireland by the sense that nation has of itself, generously maintained throughout their second-hand bookshops. I had to pinch my temples on several occasions to remind myself that there were other books about other places and other subjects, somewhere, though not in Ireland. As with every rule there are exceptions and the one exception I had hoped to visit, Kenny's in Galway, was unable to receive me as their stock was all in boxes for a month or two due to 'shop refurbishment and reorganisation'.

I should have known, when I entered the first bookshop of my trip, in Dublin, and the assistant assured me, as I bathed my eyes on multiple, truly ghastly copies of *And so to Bath* by Cecil Roberts, that they had huge collections of first editions locked away but that the owner wasn't quite sure yet "whether he was going to sell them or keep them as an investment".

* *at 2 Cornhill, Dorchester*

CAT 2
Mid-Summer 1996

Dorchester is a great town. I'm enjoying living here enormously. There are the occasional hiccups you'll get in any urban environment – the Friday night fling, for example. This is a curious tradition in Dorchester, not unlike other town and city centres, I fancy. The first and only prerequisite is that you get blindingly, nay, staggeringly drunk. You then proceed to the quietest spot of the inner urbanity, traditionally in Britain the 'pedestrianised precinct' which, funnily enough, is where I choose to locate my shop above which I am currently residing while house hunting. Once you have achieved complete and utter blotto-ness you ask your compatriot-in-lager where the next drink is coming from. The language used at this juncture, you must understand, is unique to compatriots-in-lager of a Friday evening around 11:30 pm. The dialogue, if I can reproduce a snippet accurately, pace Dr Doolittle, goes something like this:

"Woooaaaar?"

"Err?"

"Woooaaaar?"

"Uuurrrrrr!"

"Uuuuuuuurrrrrrr!!"

"Err? Mmmblaaa."

Often the sound of regurgitated liquid accompanies this ritual, particularly when that last frenetic conundrum is uttered. I often reflect on what these conversations actually mean and I'm confident I shall not fathom it before I find the house of my dreams a little further out of the centre of town. I hope your Summer is behaving itself.

CAT 3
Autumn 1996

I am writing this just after the Labour Party leader Tony Blair has sat down from delivering his party conference speech, which, I have to say, I was very impressed by, as were all the commentators who were asked for their immediate reaction. I suspect this time round we will get a change of government and, judging by Tony Blair's attitude, a government that might actually have a vision, just as Margaret Thatcher seemed to have back in 1979. It's funny how one can sense a mood swing in the country, and I do sense it just now. It surprises me to say that because I'm not a particularly political animal and had long felt that politicians were lost shepherds looking for a flock to lead. Margaret Thatcher in 1979 and now Tony Blair this year conveyed something different, a passion that I experienced as genuine. I only hope that Tony Blair does not over-identify with his inevitable coming success as Margaret Thatcher did hers.

With my political credentials clearly hung out for all to see I move on to point out that I'm exhibiting, on the Sunday only, at the PBFA Russell Fairs at the moment – until the end of this year at any rate – and would welcome a visit from any Londoners who receive or read this.

This catalogue is one I feel rather proud of; it has a few unusual and interesting items as well as all the predictable stuff. I hope you may enjoy it and feel able to treat yourself to one or two of its delicacies.

CAT 4
Winter 1996

The river, two minutes' walk from my office door, is heaving with water. The other night I took my Border Collie out there for a walk. It was not a relaxing experience since Bonnie has a turn of speed too quick for her own good. As I ambled under the stars, anticipating the following morning's frost and cursing that yet again I'd forgotten to buy some de-icer for the car windscreen, I was unaware of just how near death Bonnie came when she skidded round her favourite corner as we walked toward Stinsford, barking at the phantom attackers she persists in imagining at this particular point of our walk. The corner was deep with mud and Bonnie's flight of paw led her into a spectacular aquaplane onto the very edge of the path which was shouldered by deep and fast-moving water following the recent downpours. Sensing all this rather than seeing it, I whistled firmly and turned on my heel. Bonnie returned to me smartly, as she always does to my whistle, and we made a sedate 'Man and his dog' up the hill past the prison, eerie in its over-lighting, no one the wiser that Bonnie's side was drying a rich cake of mud as we went.

You will be receiving this catalogue in the run-up to Christmas. May I take the opportunity of wishing all my customers a safe and Happy Christmas; God knows we all deserve it. My heart goes out to Anita Roddick's daughter who has chosen to turn her back on the wealth and glitz that her parents' money could bring her, preferring to live frugally, in second-hand clothes and borrowed bed-sits. It is a comment on our times, is it not, when those who can afford certain lifestyles choose to live in a manner most have been striving to get away from. Maybe some of the younger generation are catching sight of the fact that the prize is sometimes not worth the candle ....

CAT 5
Early Spring 1997

On February 1st this year I took off in my ancient VW camper van for Portsmouth. Here I took the ferry to Bilbao, 36 hours with a choice of two cinemas and five restaurants. Within 2 hours of bombing into the hinterland of Spain I was stopped by two policemen, who ducked out from behind their huge motorcycles to ask me what I thought I was doing, living a free life like this while everyone else was in the middle of their most earnest working patch of the year. I threw my hands around a lot and smiled and they waved me on my way. This was to happen on four separate occasions during my 2 weeks in Spain. Moving on I took a ferry to Majorca, where I had a happy interlude in Deia, the fruits of which can be found in this catalogue.

Returning to Spain on a blissfully sunny Mediterranean Monday I had 12 hours of uninterrupted sunbathing on the top deck of this boat, which boasted 14 passengers, two of whom were Britons returning to their homeland with tail between their legs having gone belly up after 6 years of developing certain pieces of Majorcan land. It was a particularly moving sight to see these kind people, for they were kind, reduced from a £2 million empire to a Peugeot 205 crammed to the gills with their belongings and a roof rack piled so high it leant in the wind.

I hit Barcelona at 9 pm and proceeded to get totally lost. By midnight I was finally heading out of the city towards France, where I was to have further adventures. I will write of them, perhaps, in a future catalogue. For now I can only recommend the idea of a monthly sabbatical. I shall be taking another one at the first opportunity!

CAT 6
Spring 1997

Easter is over and now we can cruise, uninterruptedly, into a summer they promise will be long and hot. But no, I'm in fantasy land; John Major has called an election, which should be fast approaching by the time you get this. If you're anything like me you'll be getting to that state of mind and nerves where one involuntarily thrashes out at any politician beginning to form their mouth in a shape suggestive of posing a question or, heaven forbid, yet another fatuous answer.

Cynicism aside I would like to recommend a book to all and sundry which I'm not offering in this current brace of catalogues. The author is Ken Wilber and the book is *No Boundary.* It is not a novel but it is novel. It is not poetry but it is poetic. It is to be found under the psychology listings of Books in Print I imagine. A little gem, along with *Lila* by Robert Persig. I read the latter on my wanderings referred to in Catalogue 5 – a wonderful book. Such recommendations made, I now encourage you to cast an eye over this and the next catalogue, for there MUST be something here that would feel at home on your shelves. They've positively nested on mine, at least some of them have, since I have not catalogued a good number of them before, although I bought them some time ago.

I shall be exhibiting at the ABA Grosvenor Hotel Book Fair at the end of June this year. Maybe see you there.

CAT 8
Summer 1997

I have dated this catalogue 'Summer' as the first ball of the first 1-day match between Australia and England has just been bowled, indicating Summer is truly here. At present Australia are 26 for 1 and looking ominously confident, particularly Steve Waugh. Oh dear, his brother Mark has just hit the ball to the boundary! Enough of this, let us consider brighter things such as the veritably bountiful selection offered here. I say this with no modesty whatsoever because I'm very pleased to own, however temporarily, such gems as the very sadly late Laurie Lee's *An Obstinate Exile.*

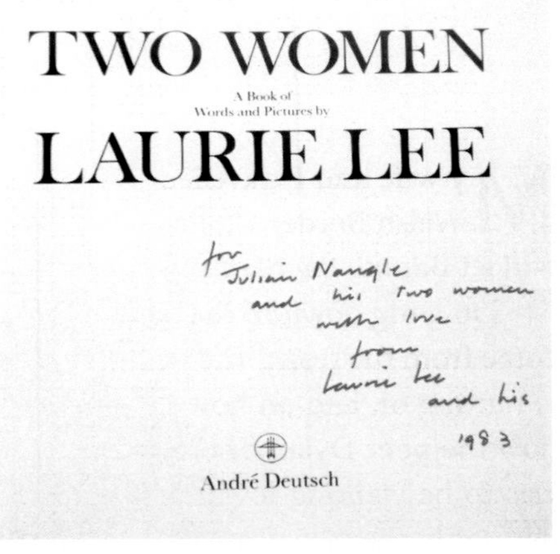

Speaking of Laurie Lee I have never forgotten a visit I made to Bernard Stone's shop, The Turret Bookshop, in 1983 when Lee's *Two Women* had just been published and he happened to be sitting chatting with Bernard when I arrived. The three of us went out for a drink at some local hostelry and, after discovering I had responsibility for two small girls, Lee inscribed his book, which I'd purchased before we left the shop, "For Julian Nangle and his two women with love from Laurie Lee and his". It is one of those treasures one cannot put a value on. So when I hastened back home in time to pick up the said responsibilities from their respective schools and prepared us a good healthy soup I excitedly shared the new treasure with my children. Alas, they were keener on arguing their case to watch *Starsky and Hutch* than perusing Lee's beautiful book, so I mused over the book alone a little later, flicking over the pages in awe of the great man. Imagine my chagrin then, when I fumbled and dropped the book – plop – straight into my second bowl of soup, staining forever the red cloth covers (I had removed the dust jacket in best 'collector' fashion before allowing the children anywhere near it). I still have the book of course and have grown enormously fond of the stain to the lower right-hand corner of the upper cover, as have my daughters.

Since writing this, both Mark and Steve Waugh have lost their wickets! There IS hope for England!

CAT 9
Autumn 1997

My wife and I travelled in Wales during the Summer, with Bonnie the Welsh Border Collie of course, and we had a marvellous encounter. I will let Bonnie tell the story.

I'm lying down in the back of the van as ever when I hear a commotion come from the front. The van stops and at last I get to stretch my legs. Julian is ranting on and on how he'd not been here, Laugharne, for 30 years and how the poet Dylan Thomas used to be his hero and how wonderful it all was to be walking towards The Boathouse on a deserted Sunday evening with only the sound of the mud hissing in the estuary and the occasional gull trying to get cheeky with me. It was nice enough, but then the next morning we were back there and they were peering through this window in what they called Dylan's Writing Shed and getting all excited about some curled-up photographs and lots of cobwebs between Van Goghian chairs that lay idly about in, what appeared to me to be, a worn-out garage.

While Anna made my breakfast Julian and I went off for another walk towards The Boathouse but we didn't get far. Julian gets tired very quickly, you see, so we sat down by this bench. There were several benches. An old codger with just one tooth sat down with a runt of a mongrel terrier with diarrhoea, attached to a piece of string – huh – at the very next bench, and Julian, I don't know what got into him, started chatting to this extraordinary bloke.

It transpired that he'd played darts with Dylan Thomas, had matched drinks with him at Browns Hotel and was proud to say that the woofing sod had been one of his woofing mates. "But, do yer know, they spent three and 'arf million doin' up that house? Three and 'arf million!"

"Good Lord," says Julian, "and Dylan didn't have three and a half pence to rub together!"

"He didna ha' two pence to ra' togetha – he couldna buy a paper!!!"

So? thought I. I can't claim to have one pence, but who wants a paper to read when you can write lines like "and I sang in my chains like the sea"? or chase silly little terriers around benches all day?

The old codger said his father used to sell fish and chips from a Rolls-Royce and was called Danny Raye and that Dylan had written all about his parents. He went on and on about times with this Dylan: how the woofing sod didn't give a woof for all the woofing this and that – just liked to be one of the woofing lads.

"The silly woofing woofer would sit down right next to me 'ere, if he were passin' now," said Danny Raye's son.

And Julian believed him. And one last tip from Danny Raye's son.

"It was Caitlin who was the piss-house, not Dylan. Dylan wasn' the piss-house, it were Caitlin – she had all these men buyin' her drinks all night, see? See?"

Julian saw, I didn't, I just wanted my breakfast. BONNIE NANGLE

CAT 10
Winter 1997/98

A few of the books to be found in this catalogue were acquired on a buying trip Anna and I made to Boston in October, although the buying of books was secondary to our main reason for going to New England in October, namely 'The Fall'. We found it to be as spectacular as we had hoped and were afforded the extraordinary luxury of being driven all over north-west Massachusetts, into up-state New York and into Connecticut by our most hospitable and attentive friends, Fran Ness and Gary Oleson of Waiting for Godot Books. We slowed whenever appropriate to take deep and lingering looks at the canvas of multicoloured foliage.

My only experience of the New England Fall up to this trip was in the film *The Bostonians*, which was spectacular but no match for the real thing. To be driven past Emily Dickinson's house, enveloped by trees, to be guided through Harriet Beecher Stowe's house by a woman who quite evidently lived her life for no other purpose than to spread the word about Harriet, to cross the back yard of her house and be shown the quite magnificent interior of Mark Twain's mansion, while all the while aware of the superb colours of the trees outside was an experience we will not easily forget.

Until one takes the time to stop and see these things they really do not live, however much one might read about them or, indeed, deal in these writers' books. I was never aware, for example, that on one occasion towards the end of Stowe's life she had to be retrieved from Twain's house whither she had wandered in order to play the piano, not having this novelty in her own home. It was reputed that her mind was beginning to go and that this incident proved it, as she had asked no one's permission to enter Twain's house but the cat's.

CAT 11
Spring 1998

Settling down to write this I realise that a month will pass before anyone reads it. I'm off to France for 3 weeks to amble round the Languedoc region and from there to take in the length of the Cote d'Azur. On my return I am confident I shall be amongst a host of golden daffodils. Travelling in my VW camper I get a sense of life like no other – there are so many things that can go wrong. For this trip the AA have told me that my vehicle is too old for them to insure, so I shall be sure to 'camp up' in some idyllic spots while I'm away, in case the van fails to start in the morning and I have the difficult task of deciding whether to stay, a vagrant with an immobilised villa on the Midi, or to abandon the vehicle until I can return to reclaim her and her idyllic spot, sometime later in the year.

Since my last catalogue went out I have become a grandfather, which has been a delight, my youngest daughter giving birth to a baby boy, Louis, a week before Christmas.

My catalogue may become slightly less frequent this year (notwithstanding the possibility of becoming a vagrant in the South of France) as the advent of the Internet lengthens its shadow. If any customers can give me positive encouragement to place my stockholding on the net then please do so, as I am poised, well poised, to do it, but find myself still clinging to the old customs by my fingernails. I have the computer, I have the modem, I have even done a month's trial with CompuServe, but still I wonder – do I want to go down this black hole of technology … never to be perceived as, or to feel like, a human being again?

CAT 12
Early Summer 1998

Awash with the World Cup (Germany are currently losing 2–1 to Yugoslavia), a deflated and I suspect defeated English cricket team (currently 25 runs short of South Africa's total in the Lords Test with only three wickets left) and with the prospect of total immersion in Wimbledon tennis next week, I have struggled, thankfully, to my word processor from amidst the thundering hooves of the horses of Royal Ascot which followed my every turn last week. Now I am here I can only cry 'Hallelujah' that I am in a position to send out not only this 'Sale' catalogue but also a modest offering of recently acquired stock in Catalogue 13. Do check it out.

I shall be away from around August 6th for my annual summer holiday, but all orders that come in over this period will be dealt with immediately I get back a fortnight later. Books are unlikely to be offered so cheaply again by me and I hope that everyone will enjoy the scrabble for some of these undoubted bargains. My stepdaughter Victoria has made her first steps along the bibliophile's path by cataloguing one or two books for me which I have not over-edited. Thus there will be the occasional hiccup and idiosyncratic description, which I hope my customers will understand.

Germany have now managed to draw all square with Yugoslavia and Jimmy Hill says we should "rejoice that they went hammer and tongs at each other", and anything Jimmy Hill says is gospel, so there. For those of you who don't know Jimmy Hill, don't worry. Truly, do not worry!

CAT 13
Summer 1998

I am delighted to say that my eldest daughter Olivia has managed to get into Camberwell School of Art this September to do an MA in Book Arts which will encompass all aspects of fine press book production. Anyone with advice, tips or even some work for her, please communicate with me.

The countryside has been magnificent during the peculiar weather. I went for a walk in my favourite woods close to Thomas Hardy's cottage in the middle of May and the rhododendrons were just starting. Following all the rain in late May and early June they were all but finished when I went back last week and the grass was higher than Dylan Thomas's house. It is very exciting to come to somewhere one knows well and to find that Nature has transformed it, almost overnight. The power of Nature, subtle though it is sometimes, is there to see.

Sadly the new Manager at the shop has not worked out, so we are using the good offices of my stepdaughter Victoria, who has worked in the shop for over 2 years, to steer us through to September at least. She may or may not be going to university this year, since itchy feet have caused her to reflect seriously on returning to Africa, where she spent a life-changing few months earlier in the year. To get the up-to-date instalment on this particular soap you will need to visit the shop and check out Victoria's very latest plans with her, personally. You might also pick up a bargain or two, so do look in if you are in the county. If you are not in the county I send you summer greetings from Dorset and hope it is as sublime where you are as it is here, notwithstanding shoplifters, larcenists and other sundry thieves with which we have been plagued, as is customary, at this time of year.

CAT 14
Winter 1998

I think this may be only my third catalogue this year and there won't be another so it feels a bit unusual sitting down to write this part of the production. One little snippet of information that might be of interest to some of my customers is that Llewelyn Powys's house is, or was last week, available for rent at £350 per month. Anyone interested should contact the

Lulworth Estate. I went down there a couple of years ago, taken by a friend who had closer connections with the family than I, and had a memorable day. To live there, however, would need greater austerity than I can tolerate, although as a place from which to explore the Dorset Coastal Path it could not be bettered.

CAT 15
Spring 1999

I have had a lousy few months and I'm wondering if I'm alone with this. Since last summer there seems to have been one crisis followed by another, some business, some personal, some health. I have sought the columns of the Zodiac masters to no avail. I even started counting tea leaves until my homeopath told me I must stop drinking tea! (Caffeine, you see, and caffeine doesn't help you fight against this, that and the other, all of which I have suffered from recently.)

So, I decided to get this catalogue together to break the mould, and so it has. On the cusp of its publication I am feeling fit and well, optimistic and thoroughly enjoying the unfamiliar late February sun.

With the June Book Fairs starting in May this year I will be found at the Russell Hotel hawking my wares at the first of the two fairs there, on May 28th and 29th I believe – something like that anyway. Maybe see you there – if not I'll endeavour to get a cheapie catalogue out in the next couple of months anyway. I have about a thousand books catalogued but fear some of them have sold from the shop – well, not 'fear' exactly as there'd be little point in having the shop if some hadn't sold, but you know what I mean.

For a long time some customers have expressed interest in the varied life of my Border Collie Bonnie. I should tell them that she is well, if a little older (nine this year), and as a concession to this last is now allowed to sleep in our bedroom, despite her constant snuffles and extraordinary antics with her paws while dreaming. We do not permit her on the bed, I should say, though I know plenty of people who couldn't go to sleep *without* having the dog on the bed.

Hope your spring is a bright one and that you may find some good additions to your library here so that you might sit and leaf through the pages beneath the apple blossom in that orchard at the end of the garden.

CAT 17
Summer 1999

I feel a bit like a fossil which finds itself re-animated and crawling out from under some boulder. With the sun beating down all around it is hard to see ahead clearly. The fossil just knows, somewhere deep within his stones, that he is where he should be, but still he cannot be absolutely sure until something or somebody pays him some attention, confirms that he exists.

Since I last issued a catalogue I have been rather expansive. I now have four bookshops.

The original one in Dorchester remains and then there are shops in Weymouth, Blandford and Bridport. They are not all full of rare and second-hand books, I'm afraid, though I have a sampling in the Bridport shop and may well put some in the other shops next year. The main stock in the shops is that of remainders, and boy are they good value! I've recently had the last 4 years of Tom Stoppard's output through my hands at 40% off the publisher's price – about five different titles. There have been some sensational art books, mostly from America, on people like Francis Bacon, Modigliani (a sumptuous volume I still have copies of), Klee, Ben Nicholson, Hockney, Dali, Miro, Klimt and on and on. COME VISIT!

CAT 18
Early Spring 2000

It's been a long time getting my head round producing this catalogue while at the same time attending to the Internet. I think and hope I have achieved some kind of balance and look forward to issuing at least one more catalogue this year, while at the same time 'putting my books on the Net'. Since I do not understand how to put my catalogue on the Net I thought I would put into a catalogue that which I have recently put on the Net. I have not got a plausible website as of yet (I have one in my brother-in-law's name which boasts a listing of three books!), but when I do get one I can assure all my customers that I will advise them of its name and whereabouts.

You will notice that after each entry in this catalogue there is a 'Stock ref no'. Please TOTALLY IGNORE this. I have been unable to grasp how to print out my holdings without it, so there it remains – next time, next time … I hope you enjoy this Spring, if you can get away from one screen or another long enough to notice it.

CAT 19
Summer 2000

Somewhat to my surprise I have another catalogue ready, although the discerning eye will see it is not over-stuffed with the predictable 'Modern First Edition', though some will be found. I have gone for a slightly more eclectic cache of books which, for the most part, have walked into my shop in Dorchester. In accordance with other booksellers I am resisting putting the books in this catalogue on the Internet until a fortnight has passed from the date of its posting, in deference to those customers still enjoying the traditional way of adding to their libraries, by hard copy catalogue. I shall be pruning my mailing list after this production, so if you have not ordered anything in the past year but would still like to receive my catalogues I will need your proactive statement to this effect.

CAT 20
Late Summer 2000

Slowly I am getting the hang of the Internet and all its ramifications and slowly it is dawning on me that it is extremely handy if you are desperate to find a particular book at any cost. If you are a bookseller it is very useful to check you are not being blaringly stupid pricing a book at a certain price (see the copy of *Casino Royale* offered here* – there are several copies on the Internet priced from £14,950 down to £9,750 – all MAY be marginally better copies or, in the case of the first, an exceptionally fine copy …). But for actually buying and selling books as one might if wandering into a bookshop I am slowly returning to the fold I never wanted to leave – namely that of the catalogue bookseller who has a shop.

I may well be proven wrong, but I have a fancy there is a head of steam building up against the Net taking over our lives. I believe the public, you and me, are beginning to cut the cloth of the Net to suit our purpose more and more. There are always going to be people who like to use it for most things, just as there are people who are going to avoid it as much as they can.

In the middle will be the vast majority who will use it for what they want but will not be driven, as I and many of my colleagues have felt driven, to adopt it as the ONLY way forward. I am really pleased to be issuing this catalogue and hope to produce another before the year's out.
** at £7,500 (a similar copy recently seen in an American catalogue offered at $60,000)*

CAT 21
Autumn 2000

This is an interesting catalogue though I say it myself: collections of Amis, Ardizzone, Greene, Nonesuch Press, Powys and oddball books that I wouldn't normally associate with appearing in one of my catalogues. My favourite book, probably because I bought it this morning, is item 97*. I've never seen this book in dust wrapper before.

Incidentally, the stock reference numbers are a nuisance I have so far failed to get rid of. Please IGNORE them when ordering. Just give the catalogue numbers. Thank you.

There won't be another catalogue this year so – Happy Christmas! The catalogue will be put on the Internet, via Bibliofind, and on my website (www.wordsetcetera.co.uk), a fortnight after I have posted it to you, my regular customers.
** Selected Poems of William Barnes. The selection made by Thomas Hardy. The first edition of 1908. I'd priced it at £75 and sold it to the trade.*

CAT 23
Winter 2000

Life is proving a little frustrating and depressing. It's a result of this wretched weather and the way we all seem to fling our heads under metaphorical duvets until the next 'excitement' on the calendar, namely Easter.

Before Christmas my shops were humming with activity, unsurprisingly, and while one expects everything to go very quiet in January, this year it has gone unbelievably so. Recently there was a survey of business in Dorchester where from a sample of 490 (I was not in it) 25% reported they were in decline, 60% that they were static and 15% that they were 'thriving'. Suffice to say that I found these figures perversely reassuring as I am not in the 25% and not in the last 15%. I somehow fancy few booksellers would be, apart from those dealing in high spots, which I have to confess I find unerringly boring. The books herein come largely from the library of the late Hermann Peschmann, a literary critic who quite clearly lived for his love of poetry, his books and his friends. I have felt very privileged cataloguing them.

CAT 25
Summer 2001

It has been a torrid year so far but with hopes for improvement. To balance the onslaught of too much work and too little reward (following foot and mouth, you understand) I have taken to a hearty discipline of walking my dog Bonnie along the riverside for 45 minutes every morning, early. The discipline (I've been doing it almost 3 months without missing a day) has thrown up some surprising benefits, the most pleasing of which has been the discreet but steady increase in my level of physical fitness, not to mention the dog's. It has also brought a newly invigorated affinity with nature – I find myself marvelling at a wild climbing rose and meditating upon a silvery trout patiently poised to break the surface of the water when the right nibble floats by. All my attempts to provoke such a display with bits of bread crust have failed miserably. If anyone has a tip to produce a moment of indiscretion by the trout – I don't want to catch it, just watch it pounce – I will receive it gratefully.

This catalogue has been a long time coming, for reasons I won't go into, but I hope there may be something in it for you.

CAT 26
Winter 2001

As some of you may know I opened a shop in London 2 years ago, close to the British Museum, which started off very well but then, unaccountably, I lost interest and energy for it. To cut a very long story short that shop is now shut and the stock is all down in my shops in Dorchester and Blandford. There is much refurbishment going on in the

Dorchester shop which, when finished, will brighten up the place a bit. The Antiquarian Dept will be moving from the first floor down onto the ground floor and into an extended basement, where we shall be having a high quality selection of antiques (from a local trader) and maps and prints. I am pleased to say that almost all the existing members of the consortium will be staying on in the revamped store, which I trust will continue to be a Mecca for the discerning book buyer. More of my own better books will be on display in both Dorchester and Blandford during the course of 2002 as the area of rare and second-hand, which I have neglected a little over the past 12 months, has swung back into focus for me with something of a vengeance. See you in one of the shops, I hope, and if not, fear not, the catalogues will keep coming!

CAT 28
Autumn 2002

I said I would be putting future catalogues on the Net and probably wouldn't produce 'hard copy' catalogues again. But then, I've changed my mind! The catalogue will be posted on the Net at my website www.wordsetcetera.co.uk and I will be placing the books with Abe within a couple of weeks of your receiving this, but you will get first refusal in hard copy.

The reason I've changed my mind is that, at last, I have mastered my computer and printer to the point where I can print out the envelope labels without too much hassle. In the past it has proved a mammoth and daunting task to print out the labels, taking far, far longer and raising my blood pressure far too high to be worthwhile. Thanks to my brother-in-law, who should be given the freedom of the city of Dorchester at the very least, I am now in position to call myself computer literate.

On the matter of these books, I have many more from this library, a truly exciting 1980s and '90s collection purchased recently. If you are seeking a particular author or title from these decades, do enquire.

CAT 29
Feb/March 2003

I am sending this catalogue out to far fewer customers than in the past as I have found myself torn between listing my books on Abe, putting catalogues on my website and producing hard copy catalogues. While I enjoy the latter most of all, economics dictate that I try to air my very fast-changing stock as swiftly as I can. So the Internet is tending to win in one guise or another. Nonetheless, hard copy catalogues have their place, and for those of you loyal enough to have continued buying from me through these fast-changing times I am pleased to send you my latest offerings, which have only recently been put out in cyber space. I will be doing shorter lists in the near future featuring some interesting holdings of Henry Williamson, H.E. Bates, George Moore, David Garnett, T.E. Lawrence, Grayson, Woburn and Furnival books and others. If you have any specific requests in these areas please do ask me about them.

CAT 30
Winter 2003

It has been a long time since I sat down to write a personal note for one of my catalogues –8 months to be precise. This year I have taken something of a sabbatical from catalogues while I got myself sorted out on the Internet. This I have now done and I urge any of my customers who have access to the Net to check into my website from time to time, as I am adding to my holdings there almost daily. You will find mini collections listed there in a possibly more comprehensive fashion than in the catalogues – for example, there are many books in this catalogue of interest to the collector of books on India, Africa and the Boer War, but, because I am a total novice at print manipulation with the software I have, I seem unable to put proper headings, or even to put all the books together in the catalogue in a coherent fashion. On the Net I manage this, however.

Thus, for the browser/delver collector this catalogue could turn out to be a gold mine – one tip: look under Robinson for a very nice T.E. Lawrence item!

For much of this past year I have been living and working in Spain. While I shall not be spending quite so much time there in 2004 I intend to visit for frequent holidays. Thus the catalogues will not be as plentiful as past years but there will be plenty of activity at my website (www.wordsetcetera.co.uk).

For those interested I feel I owe them an update on my now ageing Border Collie Bonnie. She has spent a lot of time with us in Spain which has helped her arthritic joints no end, but, equally, she has spent time with my mother-in-law and brother-in-law in England, the former of whom apparently serves her breakfast in bed, whatever that means! In short, she continues to be a much-loved, pampered hound who is now 13 years of age (91 for you and I) and still going, if not particularly strong.

I hope you enjoy this offering of rare and not so rare books and that your Christmas and New Year are as happy as I intend to make mine.

Item 551. Robinson (David)" Lawrence of Arabia" Film. Mimeographed Typescript of BBC Radio Broadcast. Transmitted 18 November, 1962. ...£150.00. [It sold to a private collector]

CAT 31
Spring 2004

I am beginning to wonder whether catalogues are viable. When I was sending catalogues out in 1972 and 1973 I used to receive a response that sold half the catalogue – minimum. On one memorable occasion I sold 90% of the catalogue. This response came from well over 10% of my mailing list. Today if I sell 10% of the catalogue from 5% of the mailing list I reckon I'm justified in issuing the thing, but the economic sense is beginning to loom like a tanker in the night over the rowing boat of faith (as Humphrey Lyttleton might say).

I love producing catalogues, but I am seriously questioning the wisdom of it all in today's climate. It is not the Internet so much as the volume of 'competition'. Back in 1972/73 I was one of a handful of dealers specialising in Modern First Editions running a bookshop in Haslemere in partnership with someone who turned out to be a shark. Today I am one of a sackful of Modern First dealers and struggling to get my neck near the top. This is not meant to represent a moan, more an observation. What I need to ascertain is what exactly people are searching for, being tempted by, musing with the idea of collecting. It can't just be the high spots, can it? If you, dear valued customer, can help me here I would greatly appreciate it. Perhaps I should exert myself more as a book searcher as opposed to what I've tended to do in the past, namely buy books I think are interesting, unusual or definitely to be desired by someone out there.

I have a fancy we need to return to the days of Marks & Co and actually develop, more pro-actively, a relationship with our customers. In this way I feel I might be able to prove myself worthy of some customer loyalty. Every bookseller's dream is to have a hard core of, say, 50 customers who rely on him/her to find the books they are seeking to collect. Indeed, in the early '70s I had such a quorum, but since the advent of book fairs, to which I have something of an aversion, this quorum has dwindled significantly. I raise all this merely as a piece of bookselling/collecting flotsam. If catalogues do not pick up over the next year I feel it inevitable that I shall rely more and more heavily on sales in the shop (which is stuffed full of collectable books as well as everyday material), the Internet and the occasional, very occasional, book fair.

My next catalogue is likely to be devoted entirely to Thomas Hardy. If you wish to receive it please let me know – I don't assume my 1000-strong mailing list are all Hardy fanatics and will not be sending it out to you unless I know you actually want to receive it.

CAT 32
Summer 2004

I would like to thank Dr James Gibson for being good enough to provide an Introduction to this catalogue. Few scholars know more about Hardy; in fact, I have heard it argued that none does, so I am honoured to have his name prefacing this collection.

This catalogue is the product of several months' work and, latterly, several long nights, wrestling with the steep learning curve associated with computer software manipulation. I have experienced a strange incongruity here which has led me into fanciful theories about time. To be writing the words Hardy wrote, insofar as I have done – the titles of his books mostly – in the extraordinary impersonal arena of the innards of my computer has left me wondering if he would have been able to write a single line if living in today's Dorset. Time heals everything, but it seems to hide a lot too, which is why history is so important. I suppose gathering collections of writers' work can be perceived as history made manifest, and in this spirit I offer up this catalogue of 19th- and early 20th-century masterpieces by one of our country's greatest writers (our *greatest* poet, in my view), acutely aware that I do so in an era of the early 21st century that flickers insanely like a lit firework, uncertain whether or not to go off.

CAT 33
Late Summer 2004

This catalogue seems to have a fair bit of ephemera, always a passion of mine, so I can only hope it will appeal to you too. I am off to Spain for a couple of weeks and will return in time for the June book fairs, which will be over by the time this catalogue hits your breakfast table. May you not have spent all your funds in London!

I would like to thank everyone who responded to my note in catalogue 31. Everyone who wrote seemed to support the idea that I should continue with hard copy catalogues. I can confirm that the response has decided me to keep issuing them and I look forward to sending you another one within a few months the other side of the summer.

CAT 34
Summer 2004

This catalogue is an amalgam of an earlier catalogue I aborted, as much had been sold during the period of its printing and there is some stock just in. I trust the whole will be of interest to all regular receivers of my catalogues.

The summer is fully with us, Wimbledon losing days to the rain, the first 1-day cricket internationals washed out without a ball bowled, not to mention the football fiasco, so I'm feeling pretty secure in familiar surroundings right now.

Following the Thomas Hardy catalogue, issued earlier this year, my faith has been restored considerably in the hard copy catalogue. I can confirm I shall be sending them reasonably regularly in the future.

Spain, where my wife and I fantasised we might live, has proven a pleasant place to visit but not somewhere we wish to spend our lives, so we are selling our little house there and will consolidate fully by spending some more money on collectable books. So watch this space.

I am very struck by how few dealers seem to trail round bookshops nowadays. Visitors of this ilk to my shop have dropped off over the past 10 years by a factor of over 60%. It would be good if the idea of a day out to provincial bookshops could be rekindled in the trade, if only to keep the book trade turning its non-Internet stock over more frequently. I always remember my first visit to America (California) in 1978 and how easily and fluidly dealers would buy off each other out there. I mustn't start though, or I will deservedly earn the sobriquet of 'grumpy old man'.

CAT 35
Winter 2004

I am pleased to offer this collection of books, letters and the odd periodical in time for Christmas. I find it quite terrifying how quickly this year is passing, but I will take a big gulp of fresh air come January and disappear somewhere quiet – is there anywhere left, I wonder – for a few weeks of meditative living. At the beginning of this year my wife and I went to a spa resort in Slovenia. I can thoroughly recommend it, but would advise taking some good reading, and perhaps a pack of cards, to while away the long evenings. Walking over crunching snow in warm sunlight has its charms though, as does plunging into a jacuzzi filled with thermal spa water. We definitely felt the benefits to our health; subtle benefits but definitely there.

About half an hour ago I had news that I had finally sold my property in Spain, a little ironic now that four out of the five children are living abroad! Still, it has been quite a long process so I feel like celebrating; I'm off to lunch in one of Dorchester's classier eateries.

CAT 36
Christmas 2004

So much has happened and yet so little. Elections and deaths of heads of state, rigged elections and deaths of dreams. It seems to me the dream is the most essential personal possession to cling on to while all about one guns are blazing and humanity's head is lost in the fervour of delusory beliefs. Some may say that a delusory belief is another way of describing what is meant by the word dream. I beg to differ. A dream is held in innocence, a delusory belief held in ignorance. The first threatens no one, the second threatens everyone. Eileen Caddie (founder of the laudable Findhorn Foundation up in Scotland) was on the television the other night chiding us gently for not staying with our stillness. She points out that this is a difficult thing to do but nonetheless worth the effort. I couldn't agree more. It is all the more true when the world appears to have gone mad.

As I hinted in my last catalogue, I propose to disappear in January for a month or so but plan to be back with a catalogue of Biographies, before Easter. The shop will remain open during my absence, however. For me, modest life in a wooden shack somewhere in France, scribbling a few poems, or just some idle thoughts, without the cursed mantra of murder being broadcast into my home, is irresistible. So my wife, my dog and I are off to lose ourselves, but not before we have met all orders that might emanate from this Christmas offering, which brings with it most heartfelt but not optimistic wishes that your and my New Year may indeed be a peaceful one.

CAT 37
Spring 2005

A Day at Chydyok

(In memory of Llewelyn Powys)

How is it I am led
With your soft eyes, across the brush
Of countryside you championed with your pen
The swell and sweep of Dorset landscape lush
With undulating ribs of green,

The bones your feet trod over, when health permitted
Your energy enough
To walk from Chydyok
The hundred yards to see the sea knock
And catch the wind from off the bluff
Chalk cliffs at White Nose, Swyre and Bat's Head?

How is it I am found
This summer's day, sixty years on,
Drinking wine with one who knows you well
Though you never met, our feet on the ground –
Flag-stoned – that your boots stumbled over, set upon
Rediscovering greater grandeur than this cottage held,
Dark eyes showing the sting
The pain a solitary path can bring,
Determined to feast on the natural, wild, life
Of which the Dorset hills boast, rife
With canopies of flowers and echoes of birds' wing,
Living in a manner you knew few humans tried –
Being, in your element, without affectation or side?

How is it I can share this grace bestowed on you,
Share, if just for one day what once you knew
For all time, still unchanged, seen only by a few;
That life at Chydyok was all a man might need?
Unless he be a fool and fall for the common greed
Of modern day distractions, those that cut and cause to bleed.

[Sept 1996]

Since published in the anthology Dorset Voices by Roving Press

CAT 38
Early Summer 2005

A couple of catalogues back I promised to send out a listing of biographies, but sadly this is still a pipe dream. The books are here but not yet catalogued. What I have managed to catalogue is offered within this listing.

Some of the books I acquired on a recent trip to America, others seem to have materialised through the open shop door.

My trip to America was something of an accident as it had been my intention to spend 6 weeks in Europe. On day two, however, my wife and I were robbed just outside Avignon, while we slept in our camper van with good old, deaf old Bonnie, the dog. The thieves cut around the rubber of our front window and calmly lifted it out! They then stole our bags that had been placed between the front seats as there was no room for them in the back as we slept. They took everything! And thus it was we decided to get ourselves back to the UK and start again, which we finally achieved after days in phone booths in Cannes and elsewhere, on the line to the Vet Passport authorities in Taunton or some such place. It is an interesting and irritating fact that it is easier to get oneself back into the country without a passport than it is a dog.

Bonnie slept as soundly as we did while the dastardly deed was committed, but when we remembered she's 105 years old in human terms we forgave her!

I hope to produce another catalogue before the summer holidays start in earnest but until then send my best wishes to all my customers.

I would like to say one last thing: I learnt today that James Gibson, the foremost Hardy scholar of his day, has died. He was a good friend and an enormous encouragement to me. As many will recall, he wrote a short introduction to my Hardy catalogue last year. I am sure there are others who knew him as I knew him and will be saddened to learn of his passing. My thoughts, as I write this, are with Helen, his wife, and the rest of his family.

Bonnie, having her passport photo taken, in Cannes.

CAT 39
Late Summer 2005

At last I offer up some long-promised biographies which are by no means the full extent of my biographies stock. If I am to get this catalogue out, however, and another I have planned, of rarer good condition first editions of literature and illustration, before Christmas, I realised I had to draw a line. I hope there might be something for everyone within this listing which is in alphabetical order under subject, in the main.

Not everyone likes biographies, I have learnt recently; it has been argued that it is the work that's important, not so much the life. I think I take the opposite view, although I know this is not entirely the correct stance of someone peddling creative writing in all forms. But there it is, for better or worse; I'm ever curious about the man/woman behind the creative impulse, whereas the results of the creative impulse are, for my money, quite often disappointing and can be mixed up with unconscious actings out. Controversial and exciting though this theme might become, I don't think I want to get too bogged down in it so I'll shut up on the subject.

On a sadder note I have to record the passing of our Border Collie Bonnie. She had been with us since 1990 and I had great fun describing her antics in earlier versions of these Personal Notes. She died of old age, really, having become partially blind and deaf, arthritic and asthmatic. The inevitable had to happen, and it did so on September 2nd this year. She died in our arms. For the past 5 years she had kept guard by the doorway into our shop and had made many a friend there, causing much pleasing comment from regulars and visitors alike. We shall be scattering her ashes in Puddletown Woods, just outside Dorchester, one of her favourite walks.

My next catalogue full of choice, traditional but unusual first editions should be out within a couple of months. This catalogue will be up on my website within a week, should you have friends interested in looking it over.

I have reduced the mailing list by two-thirds, so if you receive this catalogue directly you are clearly very special to me!

CAT 40
Autumn 2005

This catalogue has been a pleasure to assemble as it is full of slightly quirky but very good condition books. This said, there is an imbalance: there are some ordinary copies of classic, traditional Modern First Editions, like *After Strange Gods* by Auden, etc., priced appropriately. Overall, however, close reading of this catalogue might throw up some unusually nice copies of some uncommon books. Looking over the catalogue I see that one book, of which I am particularly proud, has slipped the net – I have it here on my shelf and thought I had included it in the catalogue but note its absence. I shall describe it here, as it is easy to do. The book is John Cowper Powys's *Glastonbury Romance*. It is the First English Edition, published in 1933, and it is truly Fine in D/W. The price is £250.00.

So there, I've managed to squeeze it in. Many of these books, including *Glastonbury Romance*, come from the library of John Cochrane. He had a magnificent collection which came onto the market in the Summer. I was lucky enough to get a smattering. Other dealers will be listing more expensive books from the library in due course, I imagine. Cochrane was particularly strong in mid-20th-century illustrators and seemed to have known a good number of them; he thus got his books signed by the artists and appeared to keep most of his books in brown paper bags, which accounts for the amazing condition. Unfortunately these signed books were snapped up before my nose got anywhere near the trough.

I was recently mesmerised by the two-part biopic on Bob Dylan by Michael Scorsese. I was reminded of a time when Stephen Spender came to my shop in Islington to do a poetry reading, in the '70s, and I asked him what he thought of Dylan. "Magnificent," he said. "I could count on one hand the poets who are his equal." And I recall reading of Christopher Ricks, the most worthy of worthy Professors of English Literature, exclaiming to a colleague, "Isn't it wonderful to be alive at the same time as Bob Dylan?" *

It is enormously gratifying to know that what one has long held dear really is getting the attention it deserves. Surely he's up there with Mozart and Shakespeare, as an historic figure, in the field of the Arts ?

** I have only today (16th December 2014) received a mammoth tome containing every single lyric Dylan ever wrote. Simply titled The Lyrics it is the heaviest book I have ever owned, I believe.*

CAT 41
Winter 2005

The shop is chock-full of books, in case anyone feels like a trip down to Dorset. Trade on the High Street, as everyone seems to agree, has been patchy these last few months. We had the worst August in 10 years – and yet our best September! It is curious how each year we traders bemoan the fact that business is a little light yet somehow keep on trading. That said, I believe bankruptcies are up sharply this year and are forecast to rise even more sharply.

I receive less orders from overseas in response to my catalogues these days – and even less visits in the shop through the course of the year. It can't all be the pound – it's not that strong. I wonder if we are all becoming mirrors to our computer, either through Abe, Amazon et al. or eBay; or has the world grown weary of second-hand bookshops? A colleague recently told me he never bothers going to bookshops anymore as we are all Internet driven and he rarely, if ever, finds anything priced sufficiently cheaply. If this attitude spreads, where shall we be in a few years' time? While I take his point, I still seem able to pick up the odd bargain when I visit a bookshop; and the sight of a merry shopper clapping his hands in the air with glee has been known to be spotted leaving my premises on several occasions.

I read in *Bookdealer* that 5 years ago there were some 1,200 second-hand bookshops in Britain and that now there are just under 700. What are we to do – are we drowning, as a medium for selling books, without really knowing it? Book fairs are feeling the pinch too with attendance and participants significantly down year on year. The age of the collector may be moving on. At least Tesco hasn't started training its staff in Antiquarian Books, so there's still hope. Happy Christmas to all my customers, and thank you for your custom this past tumultuous year.

CAT 42
February 2006

Clear blue water laps a yard from your feet which are easily dug into the soft crumbly sand on the beach no one but you has discovered. You stretch back in the lounger beneath a palm tree which waves gently above your head, cooling the warm air. You take up a well-covered volume which you recently acquired from a bookseller in cold Dorset's catalogue and reflect: can life get any better?

Well, I suppose it could if you added to that pile of books recently acquired from your Dorset bookseller, but otherwise – no.

There are a good number of periodicals here, as those who have known me over most of my career will know I cannot resist them. Interviews in *The Paris Review*, which very likely don't get published ever again, are unique opportunities to learn something about Eliot or Faulkner or Huxley for the price of a modest meal down the pub. I can't think of a better way to while away the endless hours of sunshine on your beach or indeed the endless hours of darkness back here in Dorset, while all about you hair is being pulled from frozen scalps, frustrated by the cold or wet and not a little depressed by the shortness of the days.

But to handle an original issue of *BLAST* is to relive the era, to feel the creativity in one touch, to see the anger that consumed Lewis at this point in his life just by looking at the typography! To delicately leaf through *The Butterfly* or *The Savoy* surfaces aromas of magnificent posturing but surging inventiveness too. *The London Mercury* is one of the greatest journals of the 20th century, with stunning wood engravings in every issue to complement the extraordinarily wide-ranging and high quality literary contributions. It can be a bit boring in its presentation – those orange wrappers could have had a few more interruptions with blue or red, but when those more colourful issues come along, as they do from time to time over the life of the magazine, one's heart jumps, at least mine does, and one wonders if the contents will match the excitingly different colour of the wrappers! Sometimes, as in the case of the item listed under Blair Hughes-Stanton in this catalogue, it does! I worry I may be sounding like a geek, but for me a rich vein of contributors to a journal such as *The London Mercury*, knowing that virtually all within the issue is printed for the first time, holds out so much more magic than the first printing of some pot-boiler novel now selling for anything up to £50,000 in the right condition, when the issue which has so excited me can be had for £10 or £20. It's a nonsense, I know, but I do feel the plight of the literary periodical needs attention in this increasingly mercenary world of bookselling, where catalogue or auction reviews tend towards the dramatic, rather as the tabloid press does, sometimes overlooking the quirky or genuinely interesting. This is not always the case, but seemingly it is becoming more and more prevalent, just as it is in the general culture of the day.

CAT 43
Spring 2006

The Internet and the moguls who now appear to be controlling certain aspects of it, such as Abe, Amazon and Google, are here to stay. What is particularly galling is that the moguls appear to have us over a barrel. This morning I received a catalogue from Blackwell's Rare Book Department and spent a merry half hour selecting some treasures from within it. I became aware of this merriment in a singular way. Falling upon a collection of Powys books, my pen was out ticking one item after another. Abandonment set in and I found myself ordering a good ten books, by telephone, directly. The joy of it!

However, with Abe taking 13.5% of any sale I may make through their good offices, a sense of being ripped off permeates every such deal I do. The despair of it! I am beginning to think the unthinkable; namely to quit the Internet altogether and follow the extraordinarily brave example of Colin Page Books in Brighton who never went onto the Net in the first place, believing, correctly, that in time it would attract dealers and collectors by dint of the books NOT being listed in cyberspace.

There is one flaw to this strategy, however; every book on the Net-free shelves will have been priced according to prices found on the Net. They have not escaped the Net after all, if you will forgive the pun, as the book pricing policy cannot avoid the dominant market place of the Net itself, unless one is totally foolhardy and ready to give everything away.

I could mutter on about this for ages, but I am brought back to the experience of receiving, perusing and buying from Blackwell's catalogue. It has the edge over the Net in one fundamental and highly important department: that of the quality of life. I rarely buy on the Net unless it is to purchase a specific book for a specific customer who has asked for it. The art of 'collecting' has to remain in the sphere of happenstance, surely, unless we are all to become object-driven automatons.

CAT 44
Late Summer 2006

Yesterday afternoon Dorchester town centre, which includes our shop and home, was evacuated. The reason for this was a rogue acetylene gas bottle which had caught fire in the heat on the roof of the Post Office, currently undergoing refurbishment. The fear was that it would set off other bottles close by and produce a gigantic town centre explosion.

The disruption to the town was something to behold. Trade was effectively suspended for the day from 3.00 pm which was to be regretted as we had at least six people in the shop clutching several books each, all of which had to be laid down in a hurry as they followed our instructions to evacuate the shop.

However, and it is a big however, it started me thinking – it may be old news by the time this catalogue hits your breakfast table but I feel the principles evoked by these thoughts remain relevant: my thoughts have to do with Beirut, currently under constant bombardment, and to all the other ghastly hotspots in the world where Man is choosing to hold that life is as cheap as fish and chips. Our little town disruption feels like a Scottish August midge compared to the flock of vultures these hot spots have to put up with every day. It struck me, while discussing the Middle East with friends who 'took us in' with our food parcel last night, that the bottom line of all this conflict is territory. Religious belief plays its huge part of course, but the religious belief, it seems to me, is dove-tailed onto the land the belief insists is 'mine'. It has been true in Ireland, it was true during partition, it is true in Afghanistan, it is true in the Middle East, and if you can call manic belief in a superior race a religion, it was true in World War Two.

So, what is the thinking behind those advocating blasting one's opponent's civilians off the face of the earth? Common sense dictates that the only way territorial disputes can be resolved is around a neutral table – this is why we have lawyers in this country – a self-styled 'civilised' one. True, when there are those who are simply intent on murdering people they have to be taken out of the equation somehow, neutralised or side-lined, but at the end of the day people have to discuss sharing and/or dividing up the land. Power has to be granted to those who are committed to maintaining this sharing and/or division. It would seem that Israel uses this as its reasoning in dealings with the Palestinians and Hezbollah. It must be deduced, however, that the 'neutral' table around which people sat to divide up the land that is the Middle East all those years ago was not inclusive enough; it clearly did not include people who felt they had a right to be at that table. It is this that needs urgent redress and thereby voice can be given to those who feel unheard.

When those in the West, and those that have some power to organise a major listening post in the shape of a very large table around which anyone who wants to can sit, so long as no weapon is brought to it, get off their self-interested butts and start to facilitate easing the unbelievable pain the disenfranchised of this world feel, then, and only then, might the evening's headline news begin to have some long-term meaning and the aeon-long habit of humans to behave like mad, hungry, unconscious savages be brought to an end.

When the town centre had to be evacuated yesterday we did not just turn up at our friends' house and say 'budge over, we need your space'. We rang them up and asked if we could share their space for a while. If we had just barged in, even with the authority of the local police say, our friends would have had a justifiable grievance, not because we were sharing their space – if it was the only space available it could be argued they had a moral duty to share it – but because of the way we moved into their space, because we did not listen to what they might have to say about the whole problem, because they might have been happier if we moved in bringing a meal, or some form of shelter, or if we postponed the move a few hours. To move in without a by-your-leave and to tell our friends they just have to lump it would have brought about a breakdown in our friendship. So it is within the macrocosm – decent respect and acknowledgement for our fellow man is all it requires, along with a huge moderation of our self-interest, a genuine generosity of spirit.

I have never written politically, well not at such length, in these Personal Notes in the past, but I am beginning to find it difficult being a 'westerner' and feel like saying so! Poetry has always been my balm against the lunacy of mankind. We all rave about the fabulous 'war poetry' that comes from the unimaginable, only experiential, reality of war, but I would rather Sassoon, Graves et al. had never written their poems, if it meant the millions of wasted lives could have lived in peace.

As a society, if not as a species, we seem totally hung up on money and death. The strange thing is we don't need the one when we encounter the other. Death is merely the end of a process. The reason I have gone on at such length is not that people have died, not even that they have died young, due to the follies of mankind's squabbles over land; it is because of the ignorance that has contributed to their premature deaths and the savage legacy that such deaths leave upon the living, especially those closest to those lost. To give up a bit of land to your neighbour is an inconvenience, to give up a piece of sacred land is a sacrifice, to give up the life of one you love is an unacceptable agony.

Tony Benn's father said to him when he was still a boy: "Dare to be a Daniel, dare to stand alone, dare to take a view, dare to make it known". With this Personal Note I hope I may have done this.

CAT 45
Autumn 2006

An Autumn miscellany amidst the falling leaves. Since I am working on a much larger catalogue which probably won't see the light of day until Christmas or the New Year I wanted to send this small collection out to remind people of my continued existence despite Dorchester's bomb scare earlier this summer.

The reaction I received from my political tirade in the last catalogue was surprisingly benign and supportive and I'd like to thank all those of you who responded.

It is heart-warming and encouraging to learn that one's views are not isolated ones. I have recently set up a new, all singing and dancing, website which I would like to recommend to anyone interested in learning what my current stock holds. You can inspect it by author or by genre any time you like.

I am adding to it daily so it really couldn't be more up to the minute. The website address is currently www.wordsetcetera.co.uk, but I am working on changing that to www.nanglerarebooks.co.uk or something similar. I will notify everyone if and when I do change it – probably in the New Year. Meantime do look on the Words Etcetera website for daily additions.

I have been reflecting on the death of my dog in September 2005, a year ago now, and wonder if I might not acquire another one. My reason appears to be entirely selfish, namely to help me exercise. Ageing really is a merciless business. The mind may think the body is still in its twenties but the body emphatically has other ideas. A dog might help bring the two together, I fancy.

CAT 46
(The first under the title Nangle Rare Books)
Spring 2007

It is hard to know where to begin. As you might observe, I have changed my trading name to Nangle Rare Books, and my address is no longer at the shop, which I sold in November. We are now living in our house in Dorchester, to which everyone is invited to pay a visit to inspect the stock, or just to pay a social call, if you would ring to make an appointment first.

Since selling Words Etcetera, which continues to flourish I am glad to say, our life has been something of a roller coaster. The plan was to move back into our house in South Walks Road seamlessly, in December, and to issue a catalogue within a month of doing so. Reality, however, had other plans. The tenants, to whom we gave all due notice to quit, decided to play funny-ball and refused to budge. It took us two-and-a-half months to force them out through the auspices of a County Court Judge!

Fortunately the tenants, considering they hadn't paid rent for 3 months, left the house in good order. The only surprise awaiting our return was about 80 letters addressed to us which they had failed to forward on during their 9 months' occupancy. Twenty of these letters were from the gas and electricity suppliers threatening hell and damnation upon my head if I didn't pay what was a sharply increasing total (due to interest) for the services they had been supplying. My agent fortunately sorted this out and the suppliers are now pursuing the said tenant who clearly indulged in some limited identity fraud at my expense.

The problem that has ensued from all this is that I have been unable to access my books for 3 months as they have been boxed up. Fortunately the new owner of Words Etcetera, Simon Rushbrook, has been very generous and allowed us to store both books and furniture in his new home (our old home) above the bookshop. Now, at last, here is the catalogue I had planned to put out in January.

Please note my telephone number remains the same, the address is as above and the website is being added to daily.

CAT 47
Easter 2007

Quickly on the heels of my last catalogue, I offer this rather larger collection. I will refrain from going on here, assuming you have heard enough of my histrionics in the last Personal Note. I shall take just enough space to wish all my customers (possibly belatedly) a Happy Easter and to point out that I add books to my website www.nanglerarebooks.co.uk every day. Every time I catalogue a book without immediate prospect of a catalogue being published I put it on my website – a real-life cyberspace bookshop. During the course of this year I hope to produce another three catalogues.

I will be exhibiting at the PBFA Bath Book Fair at the end of April and at the ABA Fair at Olympia in early June.

CAT 48
Summer 2007

It has been an eventful couple of months since my last catalogue. I have been to Scotland for a couple of days and then spent a week in London where I did the Olympia Fair and, more importantly, got to see 'We Will Rock You', the Ben Elton/Queen musical. It was like being sucked into a virtual world of preteens. I was surrounded by prepubescent children waving battery-powered candles to Bohemian Rhapsody. I blame Wayne's World – but it was fun!

Another grandchild has been born, making it eight now. Stop, stop.

I was very touched by a number of remarks following my rather muted Personal Note in the last catalogue. It seems some people actually missed my normal, lengthier ramblings. Nonetheless, I must be measured in what I say as I want to say I am astonished by the way this country is being run – the new Prime Minister unelected, his Deputy conducting a Presidential-style campaign across the country. I do wonder what these people really know about, for example, the homeless strewn across the streets of London (and everywhere else, including Dorchester). If a government can't even provide shelter for its subjects, and some form of emotional and financial support, by default, what purpose 'defending the realm' (albeit on another continent) with their mega defence budget?

I am involved locally in an effort to bring greater facilities and profile to Hardy's home town, using an initiative called the Business Improvement District (BID) which was started 4 years ago by the office of the outgoing Deputy Prime Minister, John Prescott. In essence this initiative relies on local businessmen and -women volunteering their time to whip up support from other businesses to vote, in a special ballot, to pay money into a ring-fenced fund so that their town and business environment can be improved and promoted.

This sounds like Business Rates Take Two, which in a sense it is but with a major difference: 100% of the money raised is spent on what the local BID proposal document says it will be spent on. Compare this with the fact that only 6% of the business rates paid by businesses in Dorchester comes back to be spent in and on Dorchester – 94% is spent on matters Ministers, tucked away in their comfortable limousines and offices in London, decide are priorities.

And they wonder why some of us don't bother to vote?

CAT 49
Autumn 2007

What a summer we have had! I don't just mean the weather, but the speed of life. I have spent much of it outside, which has been nice. At the end of July I helped to organise a conference/festival for the Association of Humanistic Psychology. It was the weekend after the Gloucestershire and Worcestershire floods. These floods, incidentally, affected major cities that received no attention in the press whatsoever – Sheffield is one I know of; they had streets filled with water for days but not one monosyllable of national coverage as far as I could make out – and there were others. I find this strange and slightly worrying.

Anyway, the conference was deemed a success, despite the mud through which we all had to plough for the weekend: it was held at the only tented conference centre in Britain called 'Green and Away' – very earthy, very green, very modern. What else would you expect from me? The majority of the delegates loved it, despite many of them never having camped in their lives before that weekend.

Anyway, Anna and I moved on a week later to yet another camp; this one lasted 10 days and was full of dance, music and camp fires – great fun, living in one of the 16 circles, each of some 30 people, cooking together, sharing the highs and lows of outdoor living together.

There is a programme on TV that has recently hit our screens called 'Dumped' where a group of people seem to have to live together on a landfill site – to heighten their awareness, and the viewers' awareness, about 'waste'. This is the Hellfire version of what we did at our 10-day camp. Ours was much more gentle, so much more supportive of one another, so much more 'so'.

Regular readers of this piece might detect a note of light-motif about it this time. For some reason, I cannot take the world seriously anymore. This is because it is clearly halfway down the drain and I feel totally ill equipped to stop it falling the whole way down. I am not depressed about it, but I do feel resigned. I shall keep on offering my bookish wares, I shall continue to be creative in my own quiet ways, but I really cannot engage with the mood of debate as I now hear it on the radio or in other branches of the media. Perhaps it is because this summer I also had an outdoor party to celebrate my 60th birthday. Having reached this extraordinary pinnacle of achievement I feel more than ever like saying 'sod it' about virtually everything. Do forgive me!

CAT 50
Winter 2007

I am 'listening again' to Bob Dylan's Theme Time Radio, this time on Luck. It struck me, hearing him talk about the superstitions associated with luck, that they could do with some in Somalia just now. I saw images on the TV the other night that took me back to 1985, and Michael Buerk's reports from Ethiopia. We don't seem to learn from history, do we?

This catalogue has much relating to Edward Gordon Craig, his mother Ellen Terry, and his son Edward Carrick, better known as Edward Craig. EGC and his son seem to have been joined at the hip by their interest in theatre and set design. This was taken one step further by Edward Craig, when the cinema became more than a novelty and filled the mainstream.

One gets the impression from their library that Edward Craig *fils* was able to repay the interest his father had given him in theatre and set design by introducing his father to design in the cinema. I may be wrong, of course, but it's the impression I have gathered while immersed in their library.

Some of the books are annotated by both father and son, and sometimes by others as well. It has been difficult, at times, to distinguish just who is who. I would like to thank Michael Meredith here for his help in identifying some of the hand writing. Michael is a man whose knowledge of Edward Gordon Craig and his circle, and of many other writers, is awesome. If you want to see a really impressive collection of Craig material in this country just contact Michael at Eton College Library – you will have a treat in store beyond imagining as he is happy to show serious students and scholars the collection. Where it is not obvious the item has come from the Craig library I have put ICL at the end of the description.

It is very possible I shall fall silent for a bit; do not be surprised if my next catalogue takes a while to appear. I am feeling inclined to change emphasis for a few months. So, just beneath the picture on the back of this catalogue please imagine an old Huck Finn-like sign saying 'Gone Fishin'.

CAT 51
Spring 2008

This catalogue is offered humbly in memory of my old friend Peter Jolliffe who died just after Christmas last year. Ulysses, his business name, will doubtless live on in the annals of bookselling history in Britain, and it is only right that it should. Testament enough for any bookseller, and an appropriate one for Peter.

And those of us still alive carry on, of course, and do as we can. It is my intention to engage the world with a light heart and a hopeful attitude. My wife and I have recently moved from Dorchester to Chichester, as you will see from my new address at the top of this page. I have to say I am absolutely loving being in Chichester, in a flat rather than a house, which somehow gives me a spring in my step. It's as if I am 20 years old again and 'living in a flat' – for who, at that age, could afford to do any different, other than stay at home with their parents?

Thus my new lifestyle is uplifting me in a way I never anticipated or planned for, and I thank the powers that be every day just for being here. As a result of this, a trait has begun to enter my bookselling which has also surprised me; it is that I have made a particular effort to price my books at an affordable level, to the point of hopefully tempting some new collectors to enter the field who will actually start collecting, instead of just' bargain hunting' or 'investing', which seems to have become the norm for the more successful Thatcher Babes, if I may call them that. This may be classed as provocative of me – I do not intend it to be – I just want to reach out to younger collectors who might like to acquire and enjoy some of the books I have acquired and enjoyed over the years. To this end, you will find, for example, a host of Hogarth Press books, which some might see as becoming unfashionable but which I see as old and familiar friends, intimately linked to the lives of Virginia and Leonard Woolf and their circle.

I recently saw a sign in the back of a VW van which said, simply, 'Where have all the hippies gone?' It made me reflect. The spirit that arose and lived through the hippy lifestyle is still out there, but it has been overshadowed by years of Thatcherism and Blairism and a culture of greed. I sense the beginnings of a return, if not to hippy life, to a demand for more basic, human values, if for no other reason than there is ample evidence that the alternatives of scrabbling around, trampling everyone else underfoot, simply do not work for most people. If you know the film 'Pass It Forward' you will understand where I'm coming from. It is an inspiring idea that is rooted in the film, with its source firmly rooted in universal love: something we are a bit short of currently, it seems to me.

CAT 52
(Mostly Poetry)
Spring 2008

This catalogue comes reasonably swiftly on the heels of my last. It is mostly poetry because poetry comforts me, even in snippets or single lines, when times get a little heavy, and times are a little heavy if one can bear to follow 'the News'.

This said, as I reported in my Note last time, I am thoroughly enjoying Chichester and marvelling at the buds on the tree right outside my dormer window which constitutes the west-facing wall of my office. This tree, whose 'type' I am ashamed to say I cannot name, is the only thing between me and the spire of Chichester Cathedral. Now this inspires me, if you'll forgive the pun, because I have only recently learnt of the fleeting but profound influence this very cathedral had upon the young Eric Gill.

In 1898 Gill lived in Chichester for a year and by all accounts loved it: "something as human as home and as lovely as heaven". He had moved to Chichester, following his father's new placement within the Church, from Brighton, which he found to be "a meaningless congerie of slums and suburbs, camouflaged by a Regency façade". I have Robert Speaight's biography of Gill (1966) to thank for this information.

I recently attended an auction at Henry Adams in the city and thought for a second I might find the Holy Grail of all auctions* – one no one else really knew about. Among the books were some from Leonard and Virginia Woolf's library which were estimated at laughable levels. I could find no record of the auction in *Bookdealer* and thus naively thought I might have 'a chance'. Fat chance! Dealers were down in force and I picked up but one item from the sale, two vols relating to Keats, alas not in the previous ownership of the Woolfs. These now grace the front cover of this catalogue. I hope you like them – I find them very handsome.

* *Once upon a time I did – in 1972 – at an auction in Reigate or Redhill, I forget which. I bought a boxed lot of about 20 Evelyn Waugh first editions for £70.00. Among the gems, all in dust wrappers, were Vile Bodies and Handful of Dust – oh, the joy of selling those two for £12.50 each!*

CAT 54
Summer 2008

Everyone we tell says, "You're mad, but actually, it just might work ...". Anna and I have decided to open a bookshop. Another bookshop. This after swearing on the bible of booksellers, 'The ABC of How to go Bankrupt' by Ivor Problem, that we'd never ever open another shop whatever, whatever. Well, we have decided to buck the trend.

Chichester has something of a paucity of good bookshops and, speaking for myself, and a little for Anna, I just love the theatricality of owning a bookshop; of showing the world my wares. Perhaps 'exhibitionism' is a truer word than 'theatricality', but it doesn't reflect quite so well, does it, so I'll stick with the theatrical connection.

And why not, in Chichester? There is so much culture here which lies hidden, almost suffocated, by the designer clothes shops and chic jewellery shops. We are convinced that, if offered a watering hole, the culture vultures will come drink. We sincerely hope so. There are already art galleries to die for here, there is the world-famous Chichester Festival Theatre, there is an extremely good blues guitarist and singer who busks infrequently who could give Eddy Grant a run for his money.

We need a renaissance – I am sick and tired of foul-mouthed yobs and yobettes clogging up the airwaves and streets with their lack of inspiration and imagination. I want the world, at least in Chichester, to realise how lucky we are to live the way we do, with the culture, cleanliness, cuisine and comfort we have. I want those of us with a civilised, humanistic attitude to our fellow man to rise up more strongly than ever and tell the negative nerds that seem to dominate the news to take a walk or get positive. I want dreamers' dreams to surface, not stay stuffed under the pillows of regret. And that is why I'm opening another bookshop – so there!

The Crane Bookshop, 4a Crane Street, Chichester, P019 1LH, 01243 532977– from September 1st 2008. Launch Party on Friday September 5th 5.30 pm. Come, you are warmly invited, but please let me know if you accept the invite, as my daughter Poppy, who will do the catering, needs to know numbers.

CAT 55
Winter 2008

The shop's been open for a couple of months now and, while I am not off to the Caribbean for the winter, it is doing ok. There are some weeks when I couldn't ask for a better response, but then the weather turns nasty and Crane Street feels like a ghost town. Chichester is clearly a fair-weather city and comes into its own when the sun shines.

The difficult times are proving a real challenge to us all, it seems, but my answer is to try to develop a sense of 'treading water' – surviving, not striving, in other words. If I look at the current situation around the world with a cool head I feel a bit like a boxer, battered around from top to toe one minute with news of doom, gloom and disaster, and then caressed gently with a warm towel the next with tales of individual heroism and, let's not forget, Obama.

Obama's mantra, not unlike Richard Branson's of "screw it, let's do it", although much more elegant, has certainly uplifted people, myself included.

But we have to be prepared to dig deep, it seems, and this is what I am trying to do. There are so many people in the world worse off than us that it hardly behoves one to linger a millisecond on the struggles of economic survival, but then this is our reality – we have in place a wide range of obligations, some financial, some personal – we have to continue to meet these. Thus I offer a rather overdue catalogue and hope you may find something within it to brighten these dark wintry days. And when it comes I hope you have a good Christmas, and a happy one.

CAT 56
Feb/March 2009

It has been a hard winter and if the weather forecast for this weekend, the famous 'Arctic Blast', is accurate, it's going to get harder. This said, the difficulties to date have not been primarily climatic but fiscal and mental.

The overwhelming feeling I have picked up is the swift descent of confidence in anything. Booksellers are remarking to each other that business is quiet; indeed some of the major players have reputedly stopped buying altogether. I hear tales of books at auctions being 'bought in' by the dozen and of cancellations by British booksellers of bookings to attend the San Francisco Book Fair next month.

And then I look around me and notice the early signs of Spring: the snowdrops popping up all over the place and the promise of daffodils. Some grass seed we scattered in our garden 2 months ago has suddenly appeared as a faint carpet of green. Days when the sun shines become ever more important in the winter and I have found myself stopping work and going out for a walk when the sun shines, just to remind myself that life is not all about 'growth' and 'selling' and 'progress', but about now, about enjoying the moment for whatever it brings.

This feels even more important since my wife and I signed up to our local Transition initiative. Those who have not come across this movement will hear of it soon, I forecast, as it is the way forward through the quagmire of corruption and greed, selfishness and fear that dogs the planet at the moment.

In a nutshell, Transition Towns are towns that see the importance of smaller communities banding together to action vital changes to our way of life that the greater community, run by Government of whatever colour, is failing to do. People speak of Peak Oil – the moment when demand outstrips supply for this 'vital' product – and how we are all going to have to learn to manage what is called the 'energy descent' that will be our reality within one or two decades.

These are early days in the education of the world in these matters, but very late days in terms of time to change things around. I find myself living by the mantra of "where there is intent, there is resilience, where there is resilience, there is hope, and where there is hope, there can be found the foundations of confidence".

CAT 57
Spring 2009

I will have returned recently from Spain when you receive this latest offering. I only hope the country will have settled down a little by then. At time of writing, the media seem to be full of high dudgeon and indignation about the emails coming from our leader's office.

I haven't read any of the offending missives the newspapers object to so strongly but which they nonetheless reserve the right to publish. I heard Andrew Neill defending this right on the radio this morning and found myself spluttering a mouthful of toast into my coffee. It's quite clear that a wild cat has got amongst the cream and that it was utterly correct that he retire, tail between legs, through the appropriate flap in the back door of No. 10 Downing Street. But why the Press feel entitled to, at one and the same time, publish hurtful extracts from these emails for all and sundry to see while castigating their originator, I don't know*.

The books in this catalogue are a sample of a large collection I bought recently, some of which will be on show at the ABA June Book Fair at Olympia. I am on Stand 55 and hope to see some of you there.

Meanwhile I hope some of what I offer here will attract sufficiently for you to be in touch. I am constantly being told that hard copy catalogues are still important – I do hope you agree. For me they are an outlet for a modicum of creativity which cannot afford to find expression elsewhere. If I could earn some money sending you my latest musings, of whatever nature, believe me I would. Alas, I don't have enough self-belief to try this, so you will have to accept my recent purchases as a substitute for any literary creations I might have concocted, given a handsome annuity from the heavens. I'm just not confident enough to decamp to an attic and 'write', though there are many days when I wish I was. And I suppose my family might have something to say if I was to do it.

* *Damian McBride, special adviser to PM Gordon Brown, had been unmasked as the source of emails fabricating sexual and other scandals about Conservative MPs. He resigned on April 11th 2009.*

CAT 58
Summer 2009

When people called me mad to open a bookshop last August I shrugged it off, believing we were entering a downturn in the economy, admittedly, but that a rare and second-hand bookshop could fit in well to such a scenario, comforting and nourishing as such places can be – a lift to the troubled soul.

What I, along with the rest of the globe, did not foresee was the beginnings and seemingly an endless continuation of the end of civilisation as we have known it!

Added to this, and partly due to this, I have struggled with my health this past year and so decided to ask my landlords if I might renegotiate the shop lease. To my delight they have been incredibly human and supportive and agreed, very generously, without penalty, to alter my lease so that I could be released from my obligations at the end of a year's tenancy.

That year is now just about up and I shall be closing the doors on The Crane Bookshop in Chichester at end of business on August 22nd. Until then all the books in the shop are being offered at half their marked price.

None of the books in this catalogue is in the shop, or in that 'Sale', but I can assure you there are some wonderful bargains to be had there, if you can be troubled to come to Chichester and explore the stock.

Meanwhile I hope you may find in this catalogue some treasures too good to pass up. I shall continue to issue catalogues on a regular basis and I shall be adding to my website www.nanglerarebooks.co.uk on a daily basis while ever I have the strength to type! I have many items still to catalogue and, come the autumn, I hope to have much more time to indulge myself in this way.

I should just say that 2 months ago, just after I sent out my last catalogue, I had a computer crash and lost half my mailing list, so if you know of anyone who would enjoy receiving my catalogues, do send them my details, or send me theirs if you feel they won't mind.

CAT 59
Winter 2009

This catalogue will come as something of a surprise to a lot of people. I have inherited a mailing list from Richard Budd who retired last year and very kindly donated his mailing list to me. Richard and I go back a long way, first meeting in 1971 when he was running The Crane Bookshop for Bertram Rota Ltd in Haslemere. I took over his role in the shop when he decided to go out on his own as a bookseller specialising in poetry.

With Richard's speciality in mind I have included a fair amount of it in this catalogue, but also some other collectable books in the fields of general literature and illustrated books. There are some fine Private Press books also.

In November I was pleased to do the Chelsea Book Fair and to meet up with old friends and collectors. I will be doing the Olympia Fair next year.

Meanwhile catalogues like this one will appear from time to time while I try to get the website up to speed. There are a huge number of books listed there, but I regret to say a good number of them are sold. I've not managed to remove them from the listing yet but intend to in the not too far distant future. In the New Year we shall be moving back to Dorchester, so watch out for the new address in the next catalogue, which will appear sometime in February, hopefully.

CAT 60
Early Spring 2010

We have moved again and this time we hope we may stay more than 18 months; indeed, we hope we may have found what is fashionably (and to my ear horribly) termed our 'forever home' – ugh.

Anyway, the new home is far from horrible – it is right opposite St George's Church on Fordington Green. St George's is where Horace Moule, Thomas Hardy's early mentor, is buried, having killed himself gruesomely in 1873. Hardy was devastated by the death and lingered long over the grave at times, reflecting on his old friend. Luckily he very soon found another mentor and enthusiast for his work in Leslie Stephen, Virginia Woolf's father.

The house was something of a wreck when we acquired it and so we endured 4 months of patient and painstaking renovation, carried out by a great one-man-band handyman by the name of Duncan. We owe Duncan a lot for his refusal to desert his post when many a builder would have scarpered. My step-daughter's boyfriend, Nick, is a surveyor and when he was visiting recently he gave a relatively approving nod in the direction of the work carried out, so we feel justified in going with the local rather than the London-based builders whom we also asked for a quote back in September.

To add to the newness of our life we have also acquired a puppy – a Parsons Jack Russell called Tilly. Our kitchen is strewn with unusable cardboard from egg boxes as a consequence, but we are assured this phase 'will pass'. We surely hope so.

I shall be doing the Olympia Book Fair in June so hope I may see some of you there. Until then I wish all my customers a pleasant, warm, if late Spring.

CAT 61
Early Summer 2010

There has been so much turmoil recently it is hard to know where to begin.

Sadly, we decided we could not cope with our little puppy and so re-housed her with a family of three vibrant children and another dog in a garden the size of a football pitch. We concluded that she would be happier there, which assuaged our guilt a bit.

As I write, my daughter and three grandchildren are stuck in Spain for an extra 10 days following the debacle of the Iceland volcanic eruption. At one point I thought I was going to have to drive out there to get them, but no, they are due back around now, the end of April. I am off to America for a week in early May and will probably have just returned when you receive this.

There will be/have been an election here in Britain soon/recently – I am tempted to pontificate about the choices on offer but will resist. It is all so predictable, I feel. Until we re-assess our country's role in the world generally I fear we shall not change in any real measure, whoever gets in.

The weather recently has lifted my spirits greatly and I hope it has yours, wherever you are. May the Summer prove as warming and pleasant as the Spring. I shall be at Olympia for the ABA Book Fair (Stand 109) in early June, if anyone feels like visiting. I shall have different stock to that listed here. If you want a complimentary pass, just tell me and I'll send you one.

CAT 62
Mid-Summer 2010

Enjoying the sunny summer weather, I have found it difficult, on occasion, to be disciplined and to stay at my computer. Indeed, it makes me wonder sometimes just what I could do that didn't involve a computer. But life is changing fast, I find, and as a result and in an effort to keep up I am investing a fair bit of time and money into updating and upgrading my website: www.nanglerarebooks.co.uk

By the autumn I hope to be in a position to send out monthly e-catalogues to any who might like to receive them.* So, even if you want nothing from this catalogue but would like to receive regular emails listing recently catalogued stock (I have over 3,000 uncatalogued items currently), please send me an email saying so and I shall put you on my 'email list'. If you find they are not what you expected or do not interest you, it will be very easy and very obvious as to how you can 'unsubscribe' to such an emailing. There will be a little button you would have to click.

Part of me is sad to have to advertise such a service, having, for 40 years, sent out hard copy catalogues with much pleasure and job satisfaction. But needs must – people are not responding in anything like the numbers they used to to hard copy catalogues, so I am hoping I may attract a new generation of book collectors in this way. I will not stop sending out the normal catalogues, but the e-catalogues will be more regular and more frequent, although smaller. The new website will also allow me to start an online 'blog'. I realised recently that I have been blogging for years but didn't know it. Indeed, my first 'blog' was the Personal Note to CAT 50 way back in 1985. I often wonder whether I shouldn't gather together all my Personal Notes from the past 120 catalogues (for that is the number I have issued since CAT 50) and publish it as a 'Bookseller's Blogasphere'. Any publisher out there interested?

* *Not achieved, sadly.*

CAT 63
Late Summer 2010

May I draw your attention to the ad I have placed somewhere in this catalogue telling anyone who may be interested that we are opening our house as a Christmas bookshop on Sunday November 21st (from 12 noon through to 4.00 pm). Everyone is most welcome. There will be complimentary mince pies and mulled wine. Our house happens to lend itself to be opened up as a bookshop giving onto a garden, so we thought why not? We have had two such 'open days' already this summer and they have proved very successful, both as social gatherings and as magnets for book lovers. It would be a huge extra pleasure for me to actually meet some of my customers! So do come along if you fancy a trip out to Dorset before the real rush of Christmas starts to unravel everything.

I have had a mixed summer – a lovely few days on the Isle of Wight, lazy Sunday afternoons in our garden here in Dorset, but 2 months of being on antibiotics AND a strict diet (which I regret to say I have broken at regular intervals) ordered by a herbalist I visited (never done that before) who said my constitution needed to avoid fruit and dairy completely (this included fruit juice) but that it needed lots more meat. Some have told me this is equivalent to the Atkins diet – but Mr Atkins fell over with a heart attack and died on the pavement, I believe, so I have been feeling a touch ambivalent about the whole experience.

To add to this shadier side of my summer the herbalist gave me a foul-tasting concoction to take before every meal. When she prescribed it and I asked her how it tasted she was honest to a point and said 'foul'. So I can't really complain there. But the 2 months are almost up and, I must confess, I am feeling much stronger in myself. Whether this is down to the herbalist or the antibiotics I can only guess.

Meanwhile, this 63rd catalogue under my own name (I issued about 110 as Words Etcetera, some of you may remember) coincides with my 63rd birthday at the end of August, which gives me a certain quirky satisfaction for a reason I cannot fathom. Anyway, I hope it may bring you some kind of satisfaction and that I may see some of you here in November or, alternatively, at the York Book Fair on September 10/11th or the Chelsea Book Fair on November 5/6th. I shall be exhibiting at both.

CAT 64
Winter 2010

This catalogue is virtually exclusively poetry, with some biographies and letters of poets. There is a goodish selection of 'Collected Poems', a collection I have been putting together over the past year, and plenty of periodical contributions. Consequently, there is a Minimum Order for this catalogue. If you order anything totalling less than £10, excluding postage, the total on your invoice will be topped up to £10 plus postage costs.

The truth of the matter is that printed poetry is not 'hot', but I can't seem to get out from under its clutches. My first interest in 'literature' was poetry and I had a good teacher at school in the shape of Harry Guest, who went on to be one of the poets featured in Penguin Modern Poets; so my pedigree is impeccable, even if my poetry is not. I would ask those of you not enthralled by poetry to give a moment more to it – see it as a meditation to read a short poem, say in *The Guardian* on a Saturday, and see if this does not slow the heartbeat and the racing blood just for a second; it can only be healthy, although some of the poems published as the Saturday Poem in *The Guardian* defy belief. Some, in my view, are rubbish, but then I have never been wholly 'à *la mode*' in the world of poetry. Dry, apparently learned lines which refer to some dry, meaningless object or observation never did it for me. I find 'exclusivity' in poetry repugnant, which is why I am not a fan of Pound but am a fan of Eliot: Pound, championed by a school colleague of mine, Peter Jay, who started Anvil Press Poetry, has just never 'done it' for me. Probably because I didn't go down the 'classics' route, preferring the work of poets such as Gascoyne and Raine (that's Kathleen, not Craig, by the way). Now, having possibly started a fire I am beginning to wish I hadn't, I shall turn to more mundane matters.

We are opening our house on Sunday November 21st, as advised in the last catalogue, but we have decided to open also on Sunday October 24th. It is my intention to get this catalogue to you before this date – apologies if I have failed. I do hope you may be able to make one or other of the open days if you are in the vicinity of Dorchester, or can be. We will be open from 12 noon to 4.00 pm. I will not be offering another catalogue before Christmas, so, although as I type this we are still in September (by 1 day), I will tentatively wish you all 'a merry one'.

CAT 65
Christmas 2010

Anna took some pictures of our house in the snow this morning and I thought it might be fun to show my loyal customers where I operate from. My office is on the other side of the house, looking out onto the Green and the church, which you can just glimpse between houses.

Last catalogue I said I wouldn't be issuing another one until the New Year. However, I have made a series of buys recently so wanted to offer some of the books as quickly as I could. I had to take a temporary store room, in a farm just across the road from Thomas Hardy's birth cottage, to sort the books, and wanted to minimise the time I had to hold on to it. Costs are always a factor.

I have recently had an upgrade to the website and have been given the opportunity by its designer to have a blog. He has encouraged me to 'post' on it regularly so I have taken to writing the equivalent of a Personal Note on it on a weekly basis. I intend, over time, to put past catalogue Personal Notes on it for anyone interested in reading of my peripatetic career. Who that may be I really cannot imagine, but I'm assured by my web designer that such things do attract 'visitors'. He points to the fact that Stephen Fry now has over 2 million people following him on Twitter – a delight I have never sampled.

Speaking of 'social networking' sites, I am on Facebook but don't really want to be. I got on there by mistake when one of my children did something which prompted a reply from me via Facebook. Having given the reply I now find myself, as a child might in Hampton Court maze, totally unable to navigate myself out of the ruddy place! My culprit daughter has promised to guide me through an exit strategy over the Christmas period. I cannot wait.

A good number of the books in this catalogue come from a particular library and carry a bookplate bearing the previous owner's name. The books are generally in excellent condition and many of them are inscribed by the author. Given that present times require resilience (I do prefer that word to 'austerity'), I have purposely tried to price the books at very attainable levels. I do hope you will agree and can find some irresistible and interesting items within. Renewed good wishes for Christmas to one and all.

CAT 66
Feb 2011

This catalogue offers some more books from Pauline Rumbold's* library and other interesting recent acquisitions.

Over the past couple of months I have been writing what I hope may turn out to be 'a book' myself. This seems to have satisfied my creative urge, which normally I save up for these Personal Notes, so this one may be brief.

It has been a heavy winter so far, with a number of unexpected deaths and near deaths of colleagues and acquaintances. As one gets older I find the perception of one's self changes inevitably; the body, even, takes on new characteristics, some alarming, some just plain embarrassing.

Outside of the body, outside of myself, outside of my family and friends, the one thing I find constant is the extraordinary lengths the media goes to in order to keep the level of hype and drama as high as it possibly can. Twenty-five years ago when my wife and I got together it was this very sentiment – that the media in Britain was appalling, atrocious and totally irresponsible – that drew us together. It hasn't changed; it is still appalling, atrocious and doing its damnedest to depress us all into a big black heap.

I am sick of it. I feel it is time to start naming and shaming the namers and shamers. I think the first name I will throw into the hat, as a gesture, to get this new take on the media up and running, is, let me see now, yes, Jeremy Vine (BBC Radio 2). Have you listened to this man when he is really motoring? And of course all those right-wing news stations in America – a typical representative is what's his name – Beck? Well, there are two names and I haven't even mentioned the newspapers! Fill in the gaps at your leisure. I think it is time the 'newsmen and women' all grew up, in truth, and stopped ranting and raving and trying to get us all worked up so we can all fall back down again, onto that black heap, depressed and powerless. Power to the optimists and pleasure seekers.

* *Pauline Rumbold was the daughter of David Tennant, niece of Stephen Tennant, brothers who shared an adventurous and somewhat decadent life chronicled in various books.*

CAT 67
Spring/Summer 2011

As the cover suggests, this catalogue comprises books by and about Thomas Hardy and other major Dorset writers including the Powys brothers. It has been an interesting experience compiling it as I have been thorough in the search of my shelves, unearthing items I had forgotten I possessed.

The catalogue is a 'limited edition' of 250 copies as I am not sending it out to my entire mailing list, just those of you I think may be interested to receive it.

As I write this I am aware that an old friend, a giant among booksellers, lies critically ill in Berkeley, California. Peter Howard, of Serendipity Books, has long been regarded by us mere mortals in the field of modern first editions as a God among booksellers. He has always been hugely encouraging of his fellow dealers while, at the same time, not suffering fools gladly. To visit the shop he built up first on Shattuck Avenue, and later moved to University Avenue, over 45 years, is a wonderful experience. Last time I was there I was invited to go to 'the warehouse' in another part of town. Dozens of turrets of book-filled boxes filled the 1,000 square feet in the centre of the space while the walls were lined with shelving, all of it filled to the gills with books. I think of Peter fondly as I salute his extraordinary business talent and his knowledge, wisdom and friendship over 33 years.

The Summer is coming soon, the sun seems to be shining more than normal this Spring and I am cheerfully preparing my stock for showing at the ABA Olympia Book Fair (June 9–11). I seem to be being offered books, nice books, outside my normal range but nonetheless attractive to me. I have recently acquired a very pretty 19th-century 10-volume set of Shakespeare, the works of Kipling bound in half calf, with a couple of volumes actually signed by him, and a 48-volume set of Scott's novels in attractive half red morocco. I am not offering these for sale before the Olympia Fair as I need to be able to show off just a little when lining up against all the big boys; not that my stock will cause a murmur in those esteemed circles where books are priced in the tens of thousands these days. Oh dear, I am sounding like an old hand unable to keep up, which of course is exactly what I am. But I still enjoy bookselling, which is the main thing, and hope you might enjoy receiving this catalogue.

CAT 68
Early Summer 2011

Hot on the heels of my Dorset Writers catalogue (if you didn't receive it and would like a copy do tell me) comes this more general offering. I never seem to tire from the attraction of the overlooked. There are plenty of 'overlooked' contributions to periodicals in this catalogue, along with further volumes from Lady Pauline Rumbold's library. She was a keen collector of biographies and those offered here are by no means obvious candidates for blockbuster treatment. Similarly, her collection of poetry was widespread and varied, some of it inscribed by the authors.

If you are unable to make the ABA Book Fair I would like to offer a kind of bespoke bookselling service in these times of faceless Amazonian bookselling. If you feel inclined to come and look through my stock, any time here in Dorset, and would like a cup of tea, coffee or something stronger even, then do send me an email or lift the phone and arrange a mutually convenient time. I should be happy to engage in conversation about your particular collecting interests and to see if I might unearth something of interest to you from my stock which I may not have catalogued yet. It would be a novel reversal of the trend towards Kindle, iPad, iPhone, Blackberry, Blueberry, Strawberry and Raspberry to actually meet you and talk about the books you like and the books you seek.

I am on Facebook apparently, and with 48 unanswered messages according to the latest reminder from some anonymous nudger. Facebook may be the 'future' but it'll be a future without me. I reach retirement age next year and I propose to trundle off with my wife on a long-extended holiday somewhere 'overlooked'. As for 'Twitter', I haven't even got to the starting gate and do not intend to engage with the world using a limited number of syllables, unless of course I decide to write a haiku. Oh, I feel one coming on, as Niles Crane might say:

perfect resonance –
the sound of birds singing
in a tree
twittering

CAT 69
Summer 2011

It is difficult to know if the world is a better place than, say, 60 years ago. Today the telecommunications advances since the Festival of Britain are such that if Colonel Gadaffi should happen to sneeze we will know about it, whereas had the head of Libya chosen to massacre half his own population in 1951 it would have taken a while for us to hear about it, if at all. Remember Aden in 1956? We heard about that all right, but only because it concerned 'our boys' and our interests with the Suez Canal being closed down.

When I saw the mass of people in the square of Benghazi on the TV news the night the Libyan government forces were threatening to come in and eradicate them I was all for us going into Libya, guns blazing, and my normal default position is that of a pacifist. Incidentally, I cannot understand someone like Simon Jenkins shrugging his shoulders and opening the palms of his hands and stretching his fingers outwards and asking with a deceptively naive look on his face: "Why are we in there?" To answer his question correctly I would wish to reply we are not 'in there', we are part of the UN-approved coalition that is 'in there', and the reason the UN-approved coalition is 'in there' (actually, officially, we are 'above and beside there', although I am not so naive as to think there aren't a few SAS or whoever prowling around on the ground) is because Gadaffi has not responded to requests by the UN that he behave like any other decent human being and stop organising the murder of people who don't agree with him. I am reasonably confident there will be people reading this who do not agree with me, but I would hope they do not wish to murder me for my views. Of course I have no answer to those who reasonably ask "Why then is the UN not in other places such as Syria and Yemen?" except to mutter the words 'Russia' and 'China'.

To come to some kind of resolution to the question I posed myself at the beginning of this unusually political tirade – Is the world a better place than it was in 1951? – no, I don't believe it is. Ignorance is bliss, they say, and you can't really argue with that, especially when you are bombarded from every degree of the compass by 'BAD NEWS', which, whether you like it or not, affects your soul and thus your mood; which in turn affects your view as to whether or not the world is a better place today than 60 years ago – whether or not that is actually true: and how can one possibly gauge that? I recently read (half of) a biography of Mao and the devastating ghastliness he got up to, and I just wish I hadn't; I gave up after reading about the umpteenth torturous massacre this 'great leader' orchestrated.

Three years on I have come round to thinking that Jenkins may have been right in his stance that, basically, we shouldn't get involved.

CAT 70
Autumn 2011

Yesterday Anna and I went to see the film *Jane Eyre*. The same evening I listened to *Saturday Review* on Radio 4. Craig Raine and John Carey were two of the guests who joined Tom Sutcliffe on the show. Their response to the film couldn't have been more different. I was delighted to hear John Carey praise it to the skies, as my own response was similar to his. And then, for some reason, I was not surprised to hear Craig Raine criticise it for sentimentalising the story. Like the third guest on *Saturday Review* whose name I cannot recall, I have not read the book cover to cover but know the story well. I came out of the cinema feeling I had just watched a masterclass in acting by the two leading players, not to mention a tour de force by Judi Dench. I thoroughly recommend the film.

One of the greatest pleasures in watching a film like *Jane Eyre* is the absence of swearing through the full 90 minutes. Another of the joys is that it had 'closure', the story ends in a way that satisfies. This is what is missing, for me, in modern-day politics. The banter, the adversarial chatter, never ends. I find it all deeply depressing. It is like I imagine a child must feel being brought up in a house where the parents are perpetually quarrelling.

And then our 'peace-makers', those sent in to unravel the disagreements, just fan the flames every morning from 6 to 9 am again on Radio 4. I have stopped listening.

I now sit at the top of the stairs and cup my ears singing 'la-la-la' and dream of breezes in palm trees on a sandy beach. I dream of the smiles on the faces of dolphins who pop up at the water's edge to greet me. In the context of 'world affairs' I have disappeared into fantasy land while my interests grow more and more neglected by those I expect to care for them, i.e. those we have elected.

And then I switch my mind to another childhood story and live in hope that as our politicians and their court jesters, the Press, parade themselves daily before us, a brave person from among the lines of onlookers will shout out loudly "You have no clothes on – you are NAKED". In other words, dear 'leaders', you are full of BS. Where is such a person? They must be out there somewhere.

It seems Russell Brand is presenting himself in the guise of such a person.

CAT 71
January 2012

This catalogue is the first of what I hope may become an occasional series in which a collector I have known over many years (and I have known many of you for over 30 years) entrusts his/her books to me to make a catalogue of their primary collection.

Philip Le Brocq's books speak for themselves. When Anna and I went to Jersey to look at the collection our collective jaws dropped. It is a fabulous and eclectic mix which I hope and trust you will find tempting and of interest.

Meanwhile, life has not stood still. As you will see from my header, we have moved, again. Having been ensconced here for 2 months, now we feel we really have found what we need; namely a quiet, private, English-style cottage a minute's walk from the centre of town (but without its noise) and a 3-minute walk down to the river surrounded by fields (but with their peace and tranquillity wafting up to us from the valley they run along). Our last house was surrounded by a builder's yard and what turned out to be a car park rather than a 'Green' which our address suggested it should have been. We are truly happy in our new house and welcome any callers by appointment who might wish to come and look at the stock. There are two other booksellers in the town.

It has been something of a long winter for me so far. In September I was diagnosed with kidney stones and had a small operation in early December to prepare me for a second operation – an ultrasound bombardment – to actually remove the stones. This has left me a little below par but with hopes that after the second op, due at the end of January, I may be out of the woods. I shall doubtless give you an update in my next catalogue, although I know speaking or writing about one's health is paramount to an invitation to look away or turn the page, but there we are, this is a 'personal' note so I shall forgive myself.

I anticipate getting the next catalogue to you sooner rather than later – although it will not have the riches this one boasts as, though I say it myself, this collection is exceptional to the point where I have purposely listed a few of the more ordinary books from Philip's collection as well, just to even things out a bit and to put in glorious perspective some of the collection's many gems.

* *We moved house on this occasion for the reasons I state here but also, and mainly, because the owner of the builder's yard turned into a nightmare neighbour, bullying, rude, and just plain nasty.*

CAT 72
Spring 2012

I cannot tell you how good it feels to type 'Spring 2012' at the top of this page. It has felt like an interminable winter, like most winters do, I suppose. But now the daffodils are out, so too the crocus and snowdrops, and I begin to feel a 'spring' in my step.

In my last catalogue I warned that the next one might be hard on its heels and so it is. There are some more books from the library of Philip Le Brocq here but also some rather nice recent acquisitions as well as one or two old friends who/which drew attention to themselves as I perused my shelves. Back in the Spring of 1990 I issued Catalogue 72 under the name of Words Etcetera, which was my trading name until I sold my last shop in 2006. I was looking at this catalogue recently and saw that in my Personal

Note I referred to the fact that the number 72 has much significance. So struck was I by what I wrote then I propose to reiterate a little of it here, now.

I quote: "From earliest times the number 72 has been known to have magical qualities. The original draughtsman of the New Jerusalem Diagram, which is the symbol of divine order on earth, showed us that all the significant measurements, or virtually all, were multiples of the number 72. A few examples: the Earth's diameter (7920 miles) is 72 × 110; the Moon's diameter (2160 miles) is 72 × 30; the Sun's diameter (864,000 miles) is 72 × 3300, Earth–Sun distance (93,312,000 miles) is 72 × 1,296,000". I gleaned this information from a book I was reading at the time by the numerologist John Michell. The book was called *The Dimensions of Paradise*.

Recently, at the last Chelsea Book Fair in fact, I met a bookseller who is John Michell's nephew. He is also the famous bookseller H.D. Lyon's son, and owns and runs The Worlds End Bookshop in Kings Road. So I deduce that H.D. Lyon is the brother of John Michell, both dead now, sadly.

72: an important number and a milestone I seem to have achieved twice already. Another 7 years and I shall reach it a third time, through the number of years lived ....

CAT 73
Summer 2012

I am writing this Personal Note using hands-free voice-activated technology to minimise a repetitive strain injury I seem to have developed. It is extremely exciting to be able to talk and see one's words before one, albeit over-punctuated, while not moving one's hands at all. There is some fine-tuning to be done, but I've only had this equipment for the last week or so and cannot stop using it as is. In time I will improve the voice recognition itself.

I hope this catalogue finds you well and that the summer has finally arrived in your neck of the woods. Sometime early in the autumn I hope to be issuing another catalogue: one, however, that will be full of contributions to periodicals. I seem to have amassed a large number recently. Meanwhile here are some books which I hope you will find of interest.

The state of the world continues to depress me somewhat, and I'm sure others are similarly affected, but increasingly I seem to be affecting the art of living in the present moment, which is all one can do really. The burgeoning leaves on the trees at the end of the garden lift my spirit.

Recently Anna and I went down to Cornwall on a mini buying trip and had a lovely time in a village called Charlestown, which boasts the National Museum of Shipwrecks. The village is an old fishing port but manages to moor three Tall Ships in the tiny harbour. We stayed at the Pier House Hotel on possibly the windiest, wettest night of June but were still treated to some local Morris Dancers, all dressed up in their fruit- and flower-topped hats. When the rain stopped briefly all 15 of them laid down their tankards and went outside to dance. Magical!

CAT 74
Early Autumn 2012

I cannot ignore the fact that the world is currently (is it ever not?) exemplifying a grotesque paradox. The Paralympics are currently in full swing, but so too are the wars of the world, in Syria and Afghanistan, with the menacing whisper of war between Iran and Israel and, in consequence, the entire Middle East. There are others of course: Sudan comes to mind, which the media hardly bothers to report. To cap it all, Mitt Romney is promising 'tougher measures' against the States' adversaries if he gets elected this autumn. The wars inevitably are causing untold death, let alone injury and incapacity.

For me personally there is yet more, if gentler, paradox – here I am, sitting in a lovely backwater of Dorchester, down by a tributary of the River Frome with allotments on the opposite bank to my house, empty of activity as I write (it is early) – feeling in complete harmony with a tranquillity I have sought most of my life. How can this be? How can I be feeling such peace when all about there is turmoil?

I have no answer other than to say the Summer has brought great change for Anna and myself; you will probably note there is yet another new address. I'm afraid we just got a bit homesick in Sturminster. It has taken a great deal of energy to sustain this latest move as we have had to go into storage between houses. But here again is a paradox: as we had to go into storage, an inconvenience to say the least, we had the time and opportunity to visit our extended family – we have eight grandchildren and countless other relatives, brothers (three between us), a sister, a mother, not to mention the five children. Each one of them has seen us and some have put us up for the night. So, this reinforcement of an awareness of family has certainly helped in our sense of purpose and has left us feeling curiously settled in our new home, despite having the builders in daily for the past fortnight. But they will be gone soon and Anna and I will be here for the foreseeable future, we hope.

This catalogue comes as a celebration of all that is returning to normal. (Ah, but what is normal? I hear the philosopher in you cry – yes, quite. Well, for me it is Dorchester.) I do hope you may find something of interest within these few pages. I have thoroughly enjoyed returning to the normality of assembling a small collection of books for perusal by my customers. A much larger catalogue, of periodicals, will follow within a month or two.

By the way, my old shop in Dorchester*, which I sold back in 2006, has at last been taken by its neck scruff and is having a thorough revamp. The landlords have finally realised they cannot expect a tenant to pay £25,000 a year for a dilapidated, damp, totally broken-down building (not to mention its resident ghost) and are giving it a make-over. It has stirred a desire in me for another shop, but I am confident I shall resist. If you want to come and see my books just give me a ring. I will be pleased to offer you a guided tour of the delightful river walk as well. It starts right outside our front door.

* *About 18 months before this catalogue was issued the bookshop which I had sold 4 or 5 years earlier went into receivership. It became an empty shell until the landlords realised they had to do something and revamped the place, spending, allegedly, over £100,000 on it. Now it is a wonderful cafe and vintage/retro shop, appropriately called Re-Loved.*

CAT 75
Autumn 2012

This catalogue may take a little time to read and digest if the maximum benefit is to be gleaned from it. It is larger than most of my recent catalogues; indeed, I cannot recall doing a catalogue of this size in the past 10 years. However, back when I started in the book trade I frequently did catalogues of 1000 items and on one occasion did a catalogue of about

3000 items, but this was issued in three parts and was, as this catalogue is, devoted to periodical contributions.

Clearly, issuing a large catalogue encourages me to write long sentences. I shall try to refrain. Summer has now passed and a kind of Indian summer is upon us, complete with monsoon-like weather in parts of Britain. Down here in the south of Dorset we have been lucky, but in neighbouring Somerset the story has been quite different, with entire villages inundated.

I feel I should say a little more about this catalogue, as it is, really, a one-off. I cannot realistically afford to indulge my passion for the ephemeral too often but live in hope my bug may be catching. I know one or two of you also suffer from the affliction of the ephemeral and I rejoice in the fact and hope it lingers and incapacitates you, as it does me still. What I am not so sure of is whether there are any 'completists' out there anymore: those people who simply have to have EVERYTHING by and about an author. If there are, and you are reading this, dig in! It used to be relatively common but now seems to be the sole playground of the bibliographer.

One further thing I should say about this catalogue: there are many authors whose contributions I have listed under their name. But there are also more contributions by these same authors under other authors' listed contributions. So, for example, Roy Fuller's contributions can be found under his own name but also, if he is mentioned in the square brackets at the end of an item's description, under another author's listed contributions. I do hope that's clear. To the best of my knowledge, all the contributions, unless otherwise stated, are first appearances. This is what I find so exciting and hope to pass on to others. That a poem by Seamus Heaney, due to appear in *Death of a Naturalist* in 1966, appears in *The Listener* in January or February 1965 (alongside a review of Winston Churchill's funeral), a whole year before it sees the inside of a book, makes that issue of *The Listener* special to me, and not to be discarded. I live in hope that more and more people might agree.

CAT 76
Winter 2012

Anna and I recently purchased an electric bike each. I have to tell you this is one of the most exciting purchases I have made in a very long time. There are those who argued that one should wait until one is truly incapacitated before giving in to the pedal-assisted version of the bicycle, as, they say, one must keep moving one's joints as much as possible until the very end.

Anna and I were of the other persuasion and are delighted to say that we feel vindicated in our opinion. When we go out for a bike ride we do not stop moving our legs; indeed, I think I move mine more than ever, it is just not quite so crushingly tiring and dispiriting. Now when approaching a hill I do not automatically get off but gently pull the throttle back towards me and allow the pedal assistance to help me through. True, I have had to work through my vanity and no longer mind looking like a walnut as I set off on my travels. At least if I have an accident I know no one can accuse me of being a stupid fool for not wearing a helmet.

I was going to 'cycle' to the local book fair here in Dorchester the other day but realised I had not perfected a means of carrying books back should I purchase any, as I have no panniers on the bike as yet. In the event I found a number of interesting books that I transported in the car and which will appear in a forthcoming catalogue.

For now I hope you may find something of interest within this catalogue, sent to you in time for Christmas so that you might treat yourself or a friend to a present.

I wish all my customers a pleasant time over the holiday period and look forward to being in touch again in 2013. They said that 2012 was to herald the end of the world, so I crossed my fingers as I wrote that last bit.

CAT 77
March 2013

Staring out of my window here in Dorchester, on the very edge of town, I see a mixed message. Our camper van, in which we shall shortly set off for the Continent in search of sunshine and relaxation, is parked directly outside, in front of the giant horse-chestnut tree. Both are heaving under the weight of 3 inches of snow. I cannot believe I shall be able to enjoy the warmth of the sun in a matter of days, albeit through the prism of the vehicle's windscreen. It is too much to hope we will find warmth sufficient to sit outside in our reclining deckchairs – but we're taking them, just in case.

Then again, it may be a fool's fantasy to think we shall see any sun at all, even in southern France or northern Spain, but I continue to hope; this winter, like all winters, has been a test of perseverance and stamina.

For the past 3 weeks we have been looking after my step-son Oliver's dog Molly. She is a cross between a Jack Russell and a whippet and is the sweetest thing you could wish for. She makes no bones about sleeping for most of the day unless invited to come out for a jaunt along the river. Since the snow came (and I imagined she wouldn't want to know) she has gone completely crazy on her walks, as if the place was teeming with rabbits. Pure *joie de vivre* – however, she just loves the snow, until it turns to ice of course.

It is tempting to comment on the state of the world, but I hesitate to add anything to the endless negativity we are all treated to by the media. I prefer to stay very local and very low key. The answer to the world's woes lies in the local, I believe, in the community on your doorstep – human interaction – which reminds us that one is nothing special, has no special claims to anything, but can appreciate the existence of our fellow human beings even if only by way of a "Good morning" or afternoon nod when out for a walk. It is surprising how closed up I can become unless mindful of the importance of this simple acknowledgement.

I shall be exhibiting at the Olympia ABA Book Fair this year (June 13–15th) but hope to get another catalogue out before then. I am writing this 6 weeks before sending out the catalogue due to the aforementioned trip to the Continent, but I hope it finds you well when it eventually arrives, with the Spring well sprung and with early flowers carpeting the countryside.

A NEW OUTLET!
I now have several shelves of books from my stock in a newly opened 'vintage and retro' shop called Custard Hall, in Antelope Walk, a pedestrianised arcade in Dorchester. It is open 6 days a week. When visiting Dorchester do pop in. If you wish to meet me there give me a call first on 01305 261186. www.custardhallvintage.com, tel: 01305 457209

CAT 78
April 2013

Well, I don't know about you but here in the UK the weather has been ruddy awful and we are truly sick of it. Clearly, climate change is beginning to bite. Often people use the words 'global warming' and scoff, pointing out that we have been freezing these past months. The thing is, the 'global warming' referred to seems to be taking its toll on the poles, causing ice to melt, changing sea temperatures, which means that here in northern Europe the jet stream (not to mention the Gulf Stream) is being affected.

I think that's how it's working, but someone out there may well be able to correct me if I have the science wrong. I have the feeling that we are so far down the road we are travelling, there is little we can do to avert a major change in the way we will be living in 30 odd years. I'm not too troubled on my own account, probably be dead, but I am on my grandchildren's account.

This Spring everything is late. The daffodils in some parts of Dorset still have not bloomed – and we are talking April. The ducks that live on the mill stream opposite our house have produced not one single duckling so far. I can't wait for them to do so, but wonder if this year they might be thinking, "This is so quacking awful I think I'll give it a miss this year". Who knows? Still, there is one bit of good news: Anna and I have finally been allotted an allotment (no pun intended). We had to wait over 3 years, but our patience has borne a tufty patch that may bear fruit in time.

This catalogue has more photographs than normal as I just love Eric Ravilious and think his profile cannot be too high. I hope you will enjoy the selection I put before you.

Do come to the ABA's International Book Fair at Olympia if you can. It is on between June 13th and 15th. I will have some complimentary tickets to send out in due course.

May the Summer be warmer and drier than last year; though having said that, the ABA Fair last year enjoyed blistering heat for the 3 days it lasted, prompting some dealers to set up Heath Robinson-style tents or awnings above their stands to keep the sun off their books. This is because the new Hall we were in, and are in again this year, would be better described as a greenhouse. Spacious, airy, but still reminiscent of a greenhouse.

CAT 79
Summer 2013

Allegedly Summer has arrived, which is a relief. It was a pleasure to see some of you at the book fair at Olympia. I had a moderately successful time but found, to my consternation, that for me the best part about it was meeting up with old friends rather than selling thousands of pounds worth of books. This suggests I am losing my focus, which of course I am, and have been doing, for a very long time. It has never been about money, really, at least not lots of it. It has been about making sufficient to survive – not an easy thing to do over the period of time I have been in business for myself. I started with the Wilson government taking us into deep recession following the Heath fiasco, the 3-day week, etcetera. Wilson was followed by Callaghan, momentarily, and he was followed by Thatcher. This brought in the '80s, where everyone went mad, egocentric and selfish, and many made fortunes (but not I !) And nobody seemed to give a toss for those less fortunate than themselves. Then we had the post-Thatcher depression and recession of the early '90s. We seemed to claw our way out of that only to find ourselves back in the deep doldrums again in the mid-2000s, and it continues to this day.

Now, to be more upbeat, I have friends who go out of their way to go to the supermarket specifically to buy food to give to the local food bank. I honour such people and welcome them into my fold, if they are good enough to enter it. Increasingly, I feel, we must take personal responsibility for those around us. It is no good leaving it to the state. I hope in the next week or so to emulate my friends.

One area of state help which deserves to be named and shamed is the ratio of money given to mental health. I happened to do some research about this recently and was staggered to discover that while the total NHS budget is something in the region of £75 billion per annum, only £4.5 billion is allocated for mental health. I have been so exercised by this discrepancy I might even have written about it in a Personal Note before – if so, I apologise.

When I sat down to write this I was not aware of feeling particularly political, but it is getting harder and harder to ignore the gap between the haves and the have-nots.

Last autumn I began receiving my state pension – I became an OAP. Anna is going to have to wait an extra 6 years, until she is 66, before she gets hers – that's another 9 years of working for her. I have to say, dear customers, this money from the pension I receive is not enough to live on and, as a self-employed idiot, I never paid into a private pension. So you are going to be lumbered with receiving catalogues like this until I fall off the peg, although, increasingly, I am tempted to make it exclusively an e-catalogue. I know, I know, some of you much prefer the hard copy, as do I, but the costs are becoming exorbitant. I will have to keep my own counsel on this one.

PS. If you are ever in Dorchester, do look up Custard Hall, a kind of retro/vintage shop in Antelope Walk – some of my books can be seen there. Or come by my home ….

CAT 80
Late Summer 2013

I have often over-identified with swans. The first time I did this was years ago when I got together with Anna and we somehow found ourselves with a family of five little children. Swans often have a family of five little children and will gracefully 'swan' down the river with them, usually in single file behind them. They would appear to have not a care in the world, letting the little darlings forage for food, while they, the adults, survey the banks of the course of their lives for easy prey, such as bread. Of course what the untrained eye can't make out is that beneath the surface these swans are paddling like mad against the current, stressed beyond imaginings not to be swept back the way they came. Perhaps I over-state my case. Currently, pun intended, I do not feel 'stressed beyond imaginings', but way back, when first Anna and I found ourselves with this step family responsibility, there were levels of stress experienced which the untrained eye will not have noticed in these Personal Notes. Now, unlike the swans in this particular example, I seem to know how to glide down the river course of life, with the current, not against it.

This year, on the river that runs just outside our front door, the pair of swans had ten little cygnets, grey as smoke and graceful as floating leaves, all gliding down the river the wrong way. They were a marvel to behold and I have spent plenty of idle minutes watching them, wondering how they keep this fabulous composure while all about them seems to be falling apart (there have been noisy 'road works' on the river path this year). It strikes me again, in a more global sense, years after I first identified with it, that here is a wonderful metaphor for modern life. The world is falling apart, but life goes on in little corners of it apparently oblivious, apparently serenely untroubled.

CAT 81
Autumn 2013

This catalogue is a one-off for several reasons. For one, it represents a passion of mine. I just love the fact that most of the contributions to be found here represent their very first printing and yet, so often, are found to be less expensive than their first appearance in book form. Ernest Hemingway's *The Old Man and the Sea* (item 138)* is a good example.

Another reason for this being a 'one-off' is that none of the items listed here is on the Internet in any shape or form – not on my website nor on Abe. The only access to this stock is through what you are looking at now, be it the e-version or the hard copy version. If you are receiving the e-version and would like the hard copy version (only a few people opted to pay the £10 annual sub advertised a few catalogues ago), then I would ask for a payment of 6 first-class stamps if you live in Britain or a £5 note (or equivalent) from anyone overseas.

One important point: in the Index you will see all the authors listed and the numbers of the items in the catalogue where they feature, one way or another. If the number is in square brackets [...] this means there is an article ON the author. If the number is not in square brackets then it means there is a contribution BY the author.

If I may I would like to draw your attention to the 'by-line' at the top of this page which states there is a minimum order for this catalogue of £10.00. This means that if what your order amounts to comes to less than £10.00 I shall 'upgrade' the cost of your order to £10.00. If you order several items that are sold and there is one remaining, valued at, say, £5.00, I regret I shall still do this. It might be an idea therefore, to give me a few 'alternatives' should your first choice(s) be sold.

I very much hope you will find the catalogue interesting and enjoyable. I hope too that any bibliographers out there may find the contents helpful. I have loved putting it together, even at the expense of logical, sound business sense.

* *In Life magazine*

CAT 82
Winter 2013

I have recently finished reading a biography of Nina Hamnett by Denise Hooker. It is a remarkable tale of a woman who clearly impressed her peers when she started painting and drawing. She befriended everyone, from Augustus John to Roger Fry, and included in her coterie, of course, one of my favourite artists of the time, Henri Gaudier Brzeska. It was his sculpture of her torso that led her to title her autobiography *Laughing Torso*. Hamnett's decline into alcoholism through her love of café society, both in Paris and London, is well charted in the book. Modigliani became a particular friend in Paris. She would always buy one of the sketches he was offering every morning for 3 or 4 francs, whenever she had the spare cash. Her tragic end, falling from a window of her flat four floors up, was as inevitable as her next drink.

I find it salutary to read of people in whom I have been 'dealing' these past 40 years. It is good to be informed of, or reminded of, the reality of the lives these extraordinary people lived. I think, probably, in the modern age, the world of rock music has its parallels with the life of the artists at the beginning of the 20th century.

I hope all my customers have a pleasant, peaceful Christmas and a good New Year. 2014 is the 100th anniversary of the birth of Dylan Thomas, another of the Fitzrovia crowd, so we shall doubtless be seeing plenty of re-runs of *Under Milk Wood*, not to mention some *Arena*-style programmes on the man himself.

It was in 1967, I was living in Paris at the time, that I first read a biography of Thomas by Constantine Fitzgibbon. I laughed so loud and so long at this extraordinary life that I became a fan instantly and started collecting him as soon as I had the chance. Ten years later, in need of cash to support my fledgling business, I sold my collection to an American collector, lock, stock and barrel. I remember I had a pencil manuscript of Dylan's, of a poem by Wordsworth. He always said that to properly 'know' a poem he had to write it down. Here was the proof: a poem he was doubtless due to read on the BBC for the radio producer Douglas Cleverdon, in one of his programmes. My connection to Thomas was further sealed by the fact that Douglas, through mere chance of shared acquaintance, happened to become my mentor in my early days of bookselling. I remember he told me "Never try to sell new books as well as rare and second-hand ones – it never works". I am afraid I ignored this advice 30 years later when I was running a small chain of shops, at the height of the 'remainder' feast.

CAT 83
February 2014
The Cat and the Kind Horticulturalist

The ducks seem happy waddling along the bank of the swollen river 20 yards away from our house, so at least something positive can be taken from the scene I contemplate, staring out of my Sunday window. The rain is pouring down in a grey steel mist. There are swans, ducks and waders scattered over the water meadows beyond the allotments, upon which, until only a couple of months ago, a tabby cat called variously Lottie, Toby and Lazy Bones lived. He/she lived there for 9 years, a runaway from a house not half a mile away whose owners had made many attempts to re-domesticate him, but he wouldn't have it and returned persistently, so that eventually Lazy Bones, the name by which Anna and I came to know him (we decided he was male after considerable discussion), was left to live amidst his chosen surroundings.

Each time I went to the allotment he would come running, meowing, sometimes from as far away as 200 yards, not for food – he had a kind and generous attendant horticulturalist who would leave him milk and food periodically. The horticulturalist had also made up a cosy home for him out of pallets and spare bits of carpet left over from abandoned allotments. So no, Lazy Bones came meowing to us not requesting food but a little sit down on a lap. I always obliged as he was the sweetest tabby and seemed eternally grateful for the warmth of my lap and the lightness of my hand on his back. He would start purring the minute he landed on me. I learnt something from him actually; to allow myself that little bit of extra time to just sit and cogitate upon the wonders of growing veg. The digging I had gone across to the allotment to do could always wait just a few more minutes. And it was always only just a few minutes, as Lazy Bones did not complain when I unceremoniously stood up, obliging him to jump down, at which point, without fail, he would raise his leg and bend his back to clean himself, thoroughly. He rarely if ever complained about the brevity of his stay on the lap.

Sadly, 2 months ago, a notice went up on the gates to the allotments, literally the day after I had last sat with him, saying that Lazy Bones had been found dead, curled up on his bed in his cosy home, having suffered what the notice suggested was a heart attack. He was buried by the kind horticulturalist close to his allotment. After the burial the heavens opened and have not closed yet.

CAT 84
Spring 2014

With this catalogue I am enclosing a 'free pass' to the ABA International Book Fair at Olympia, to as many customers as I can who abide in the UK. I hope you may feel able to use it. If you do manage to get to London you will find me on stand J07. I shall have plenty more treasures in addition to those listed here, as well as some that may remain unsold from the catalogue.

Recently I purchased a large collection of books that came from the library of the late Patrick Garland. Many of these books can be found in the catalogue, but I have still more to attend to and catalogue in due time.

Patrick was a customer of mine for over 30 years, so a good number of the books have passed through my hands before. He once joked with me that he could buy an entire catalogue of my books if he had the space to house them and the money to pay for them, as our taste seemed to coincide. This is very true. Our tastes did and do coincide and I think this catalogue bears witness. There is plenty of poetry but also lots of biography and some illustrated works, all subjects close to my heart.

The observant may have noticed I have a new address at the masthead of this page. Please send all future correspondence to this address. Thank you. The phone number, email and website addresses remain the same.

I trust your Easter break has been an enjoyable, nay, a glorious one. Anna's and mine has been most pleasant, holidaying, as the Paul McCartney song tells it, 'in a cottage on the Isle of Wight'.

CAT 85
Summer 2014

June in France. Have to recommend it; the fields were golden and the roads were clear. I have been to France many times, even lived there for a time, but I had not spent the month of June there before and found it at its most beautiful.

Back to the books now and I'm pleased to offer a catalogue of signed and inscribed volumes. I trust your Summer will be an exceptional one and that the madness that continues to descend on us through the various media does not get you down. For my part I am finding it more and more difficult not to fantasise about going 'off grid'.

One of my daughters recently awoke at 6.00 am in her bedroom, she lives alone with her son, to find a man holding a bottle in his hand, off his head on drugs and drink. Can one imagine a scenario much worse while still breathing? She handled it well and managed to usher him onto a small sun terrace she has, locked the door onto it, and called the police. What did the police do? They arrived in good time but then proceeded to ask my daughter what she would like to do about it. Still in shock, she didn't know what to say and the police took the man out of the house, saying "Well, he hasn't really done anything, has he, so I don't think we will charge him, unless you wish to bring charges, miss?". As I say, my daughter was still in shock and said the first thing that came into her head – namely that she just wanted the whole incident to be over and done with.

The fact that he had managed to steal his way into her house by dint of there being a window open on the very top floor (the house has five floors, each with a single room on it) does not seem to have constituted a criminal act in the eyes of the police: altogether an alarming and at the same time a depressing thought, so, however hot it gets, keep those windows closed if you're in the city!

CAT 86
Late Summer 2014

I am looking forward to going to York Book Fair later in September – not as exhibitor but as punter. I often find interesting things there and would recommend it to anyone considering visiting. In November, however, I shall be at the ABA's Chelsea Book Fair as an exhibitor and hope to have some irresistible items on offer.

Meanwhile I submit to you this catalogue of recently acquired and/or discovered books and ephemera. I am finding an increasing attraction for ephemera as (1) it is, by definition, ephemeral and fluffy, and I like that, and (2) it takes up hardly any shelf space at all, and I like that too.

This year is my 40th anniversary as an independent bookseller and I am in the final stages of trying to organise a selected collection of the Personal Notes I've written as preface to my catalogues over the past 30 years. I started writing them in 1985. Once I have finalised my selection and before I present it to my printer, I shall show it to an editor (and I have one lined up, amazingly), who can murder all my darlings and provide me with something I might feel able to put my name to on the title page. Ideally I should get the 'book' out this year in celebration of the 40-year thing, so I must get my skates on. However, if any of you reading this would be interested in receiving a copy of said proposed book, do, please, let me know, as this will influence the number of copies I get printed. I can guarantee that such a book will not cost more than £10.00 and it may be a fair bit less – subscribe away and I might even manage, à *la* old days, a 'list of subscribers' at its end. Depends how many I get, I suppose.

Self-promotion is a dangerous art and one I am very wary of, preferring to place the plate of sweets 'out there' and see who wants to choose one, rather than throw them down people's throats. The hard sell has never been my thing really, but on this occasion I feel I have to let the world know that, yes, I am going to try to get a little book together! So there we are – I've done it!

CAT 87
Winter 2014

I have discovered something quite interesting. Seagulls suffer from, or enjoy, manic behaviour patterns. During the summer months, June through to August, their behaviour is akin to someone discovering their most prized possession is about to fall beneath the wheels of a 10-ton truck – squawking wildly as soon as the sun shows an eyebrow over the horizon. Of course, this is the breeding season. During other months, such as now in November, they sit imperiously upon their chimney stacks, barely moving, observing us all emulate their summer behaviour, ongoingly. Occasionally, when the mood takes them, they will catch a thermal and glide gracefully above, being sure to relieve themselves accurately upon parked cars beneath.

While we should not and do not resort to this kind of behaviour latterly described in the last sentence, I do feel we could learn from the seagull's culture. Perhaps we could designate 3 months of the year to racing around, warring wherever we wish, but for the rest of the year sit back, quietly, and take in what Kahlil Gibran calls our 'seafaring soul' – our 'rudder and sails being reason and passion'.

Meanwhile I would like to wish all my customers a very Happy Christmas and, if not too premature, a New Year you will be happy to live through. I have decided to try to take each new year more easily than the preceding one, thus weaning myself off life in a controlled and pleasant manner, as the years tick by.

SUBSCRIBERS

Rita Atkinson
Michael Bennett
Robert Bertram
Ali & Giles Bird
Broadhursts of Southport
Jeremy &Anthea Carver
Don & Shelia Cawthron
Mike Clement
Michael Coupe
Nick Dennys
Gordon Dent
Peter Dewes
James Fergusson
Keith Fletcher
Harriet Foges
Jean Foster
Keir& Karen Francis
Robert Galeta
Alan Gill
Pat and Paul Gillett
David Goggin
Dr Selwyn Goodacre
L.Hamshere
Laurie Hardman
Judy Hickey
Mark Hinchliffe
Lucy Howen
Robert Kidby
Colin Knowles
Jonathan Kooperstein
Edward Krawitt
Philip and Sally Le Brocq
Olivia Marchant
Michael Meredith
Prof Lawrence Mitchell
Olivia Moune
Julie & Tim Musk
Mike Nixon
Anna Nangle
Poppy Nangle
Stephen Oliver-Jones
Michael O'Sullivan
Bernard Palmer
Prof David Patterson
Gillian Patterson
Kevin Perryman
Sebastian Prentis
George Ramsden
Jon Richardson
Rickaro Books
Benedict Room
Oliver Room
Victoria Room
John Saumarez Smith
Megan Slade
Stefan Slater
James Vollmar
Richard V. Wells
Geoffrey Winch
John Windle
York Harbor Books
Zimnol Books